HEY GOD, DO YOU VALIDATE?

DISCOVER YOUR PURPOSE.
DEVELOP YOUR PLAN.
DOUBLE YOUR TALENTS.

KEVIN McBROOM

I would like to dedicate this book to the women in my life—
My mom for praying for me,
my sisters for praising me and
my wife for putting up with me.

• • •

I would also like to thank these men who helped me to discover how to
live like a five-talent servant, Oakley Gaw, Bobby Brock, Joe McGee,
Mike Campbell, and the best friend a man could ever hope for, Bob Sotis.

• • •

Romans 12:9-13

FOREWORD

Have you ever been around someone who always seems to know the right questions to ask to take things to a deeper level? I remember when I was first introduced to Kevin McBroom. It was his interview for acceptance into Author Academy Elite. AAE is a place where aspiring authors come to get the tools needed to publish and market their books. These interviews are an opportunity for me and my team to make sure AAE is a good fit for the people interested in our program. My interview with Kevin was somewhat out of the norm, however. Because the interviewer became the interviewee. Kevin was more interested in who I was as a person than how I could help him become an author. Who does that?

If you spend much time with me, sooner or later you'll hear me say *clarity attracts, confusion repels*. Kevin is definitely clear about where he's headed. He knows how he's going to get there, and why it's crucial he reaches his destination. But it wasn't always that way. Not too many years ago, Kevin was lost. His life was in shambles. He had no direction. He lacked purpose. Then, early one morning, Kevin asked God a question and guess what? God answered him. Now, it wasn't exactly what Kevin was hoping to hear. Actually, far from it. He could have answered God back and said something like, "Thanks God. I'll see what I can figure out." But if that were the case, this would be the end of the story. Instead, Kevin said, "Okay God, I'll do it. But, show me how." In his book *Hey God, Do You Validate?*, Kevin shares what

God shared with him, so as the title says, you too can *discover your purpose, develop your plan, and double your talents.*

Each year, hundreds of folks gather for our Igniting Souls Conference in my hometown of Columbus, Ohio. I like to remind the Igniting Souls Tribe to *show up filled up.* It means when you have an opportunity to be around others, you don't walk in saying *what's in it for me.* Rather, you show up prepared to focus on the needs of those around you. Kevin attends every year, and each day of the conference, his goal is to find at least one person he can serve on a deeper level. That's what I love about Kevin—he's a true servant. This past year, long after the 400-plus attendees had left the event, Kevin was still there, tearing down displays with my team and helping load them into our van because he understood how tired we all were and how much we wanted to get home to our families.

That's also why Kevin took the time to write down what God shared with him—to serve you. Now, I'll be honest, it's rarely easy figuring out God's plan for your life. It often requires making sacrifices so you can work on yourself. For me, that means getting up so early it's still dark outside. But you know, sometimes you've got to show up in the darkness so you can stand in the light.

If life no longer excites you or you feel like you're supposed to be a part of something bigger than yourself, I want to challenge you to read *Hey God, Do You Validate?.* This book will help you find the clarity you'll need if you want to live a life of significance and impact. With the tools found in this book, you'll achieve the clarity you need to change the world around you for generations to come. You know how awesome it feels when your Dad tells you you've done a good job and he's proud of you. Well, it's even cooler when God tells you. Thanks Kevin for equipping us to become history-makers and receive that ultimate pat on the back for a job well done.

Kary Oberbrunner,
Wall Street Journal and USA Today bestselling author of 12 books,
CEO of Igniting Souls.

Table of Contents

Prologue xi

Introduction xiii

Matthew 25 Scriptures xix

Part I - Felonies to Funerals

Chapter 1 - I Hate Camping 3

Chapter 2 - The Demerit 6

Chapter 3 - The Book I Didn't Read That Changed My Life 10

Chapter 4 - Poor Dad 15

Chapter 5 - Rich Dad 18

Chapter 6 - My Favorite Story 22

Chapter 7 - Lost in America 26

Chapter 8 - The Call and the Calling 32

Part II - Aptitude to Astronauts

Chapter 9 - Ass-Whoopin' or Ice Cream 39

Chapter 10 - The Five-Talent Man 43

Chapter 11 - That Boy's Got Talent 47

Chapter 12 - God-Given Gifts 51

Chapter 13 - I'm Mean 56

Chapter 14 - Just the Way I'm Wired 61

Chapter 15 - Apollo 13 Engineering 66

Part III - Purpose to Passion

Chapter 16 - The One Thing—Well, Two Things—No, Actually Three 73

Chapter 17 - Don't Step in #2 While Taking Care of #1 79

Chapter 18 - Matthew and the Hurricane 83

Chapter 19 - Teach a Man to Fish and His Wife Will Never See Him Again. . 87

Part IV - Fear to Faithfulness

Chapter 20 - It's a Wonderful, Slightly Terrifying Life 93

Chapter 21 - Wicked, Lazy and Afraid 97

Chapter 22 - Put Your Behind in Your Past 101

Chapter 23 - Baby Steps and Belly Flops 106

Chapter 24 - Two-Talent Pam 110

Chapter 25 - Five-Talent Faith 116

Part V - Gong Show to Talent Show

Chapter 26 - Here Comes the Judge 123

Chapter 27 - Only Fools Rush In 127

Chapter 28 - Doubling Your Talents 131

Chapter 29 - Looking Out for #1 137

Chapter 30 - Work is Not a Four-Letter Word 144

Chapter 31 - Talent Show 150

Applications

Application I - Spiritual Talents 157

Application II - Who Do You Love? 163

Application III - Thinking Bigger 169

Application IV - Your Best Life 175

Application V - Your "Well Done" Plan 178

Additional Resources

A Blessing 187

Five Steps to Five-Talent Faith 189

Jesus? 191

Notes 193

References 199

About the Author 203

Prologue

"Mary, I know what I'm gonna do tomorrow and the next day and the next year and the year after that. I'm shaking the dust of this crummy little town off my feet, and I'm gonna see the world; Italy, Greece, the Parthenon, the Coliseum. Then I'm coming back here and go to college and see what they know, and then I'm going to build things. I'm gonna build airfields. I'm gonna build skyscrapers a hundred stories high. I'm gonna build bridges a mile long." George Bailey - *It's a Wonderful Life*

My favorite holiday movie, *It's a Wonderful Life* by Frank Capra, may just be my favorite movie, period. The film traces the life of George Bailey, played by Jimmy Stewart. Like so many twenty-year-olds, George Bailey was full of dreams, full of hope, and full of potential. He wanted to travel the globe, build things, and change the world. But the world had something to say about that. George's well-laid plans would be altered by an unexpected death, an unforeseen war, and unplanned love.

By the standards of most, George went on to lead a wonderful life. But his longing to explore and build things larger than life was repeatedly put on hold to help others achieve their dreams. And since changing the world no longer seemed like a possibility, George had to settle for raising a family and hoping that he might one day live out his dreams through the accomplishments of his children.

On the outside, George Bailey's life was indeed wonderful. But on the inside, he felt imprisoned. George hadn't given up on his dreams—at least not entirely. He enjoyed his wonderful life, but he felt *tied down*. His responsibilities not only obligated him, but they also represented everything he looked upon as trivial. Although he would never admit it, his heart was filled with jealousy as he watched friends and family achieve what he defined as success.

God created him for greatness—he was sure of it. But his wonderful life in Bedford Falls seemed worlds apart from the life he had dreamed of living. He had had very different plans. He knew what he was going to do "tomorrow and the next day and the next year and the year after that."

Then, one day, as the old saying goes, *life happened.* On that fateful day, George's hopes and dreams, and even his faith, were put to the test. His uncle misplaced the deposit for their savings and loan business, and the mistake was discovered by a board member and villain in the movie, Mr. Potter. Potter sets into motion for George to be charged with embezzlement and fraud.

George is about to exchange his life, where he felt imprisoned, for a real-life prison. With no hope in sight, George walks onto a bridge, stares down at the icy waters below, and begins to pray as he contemplates suicide, "Show me the way, Lord. Show me the way."

I love this movie because I identify so strongly with the struggles of George Bailey. This movie gives me hope. It strengthens my faith. Like George, I also had plans but traded my childhood dreams for a "wonderful life." I also questioned my path and faced overwhelming circumstances. And yes, I even battled the demons of suicide.

This scene on the bridge is where the movie begins. The bits described above are scattered throughout the film as flashbacks. Most of you probably know what happens. God sends George help in the form of a misfit angel named Clarence. As Clarence tries to comfort him, George snaps and says, "I wish I'd never been born."

"Okay," says Clarence. "You've got your wish. You've never been born."

Wouldn't it be incredible to see how our day-to-day choices impact the future? George got to see what things would have been like if he had never existed. He was surprised to learn that even though his life was nothing like he'd hoped for, his selflessness had significantly impacted *his* world and the lives of the people who were a part of it.

That's probably why the film is loved by so many. It reminds us that though we may view our lives as unimportant and insignificant, we each have the ability to live a wonderful life by putting the needs of others before our own. So, if you think your words and actions have little impact on the lives of others, I'm here to disagree with you. I believe God has given each of us the talents needed to literally shape the course of history.

Introduction

For many years, I have asked prospective employees to fill out a "questionnaire" before being considered for an interview. Honestly, I skim over the answers more than I probably should. But there is one question I never skip. The answer to this question allows me to understand the applicant on a more personal level. This question opens the door to deeper, more intimate conversations than the typical work-related psychobabble—"If you could change one thing from your past, what would it be?"

Of course, I must remember that these individuals are trying to impress me in hopes of getting a job offer. But most of the time, I think I get a truthful, introspective answer. The most common is, "I would have stayed in school" or some derivative of that statement. This answer is followed in popularity by, "I would have waited to get married." These two answers account for at least 50% of all applicants. If they make it to the interviewing stage, I remind them of their answer and ask one additional question. "Did anyone tell you they felt you were making the wrong decision, and if so, why didn't you follow their advice?"

Like me, you've most likely suffered through the consequences of poor decision-making, and chances are, on numerous occasions, someone tried to warn you that you were about to make a mistake. We don't like to listen to advice, do we? In a way, this book is a form of advice. I wrote it hoping others wouldn't have to endure the same hardships I've faced. I wouldn't wish what I've been through on anybody, even though I know a few people who deserve it. Regardless, I'm guessing there are enough people in the world who could benefit from what I've learned. So, I think you could say I felt compelled to offer some "advice" to anyone willing to listen.

Now, chances are, you don't know anything about me. It's hard for me to take advice from a stranger, and the same is probably true for you. So, let me pose a few questions to help you decide if this book is right for you.

I know this sounds cliche, but do you ever wonder if there's more to life? Would you describe your life as exciting, or for the most part, does it all seem a bit trivial? Do you ever feel like you're supposed to be a part of something bigger? Maybe something so important it will impact future generations? Wait, I'm not finished.

Have you ever wondered why God made you the way you are? Was it on purpose? Did He create you *for* a purpose? Is it possible there's some divine plan for your life, and you're missing it? If so, how are you supposed to know what it is? And what if, like George Bailey in the movie *It's a Wonderful Life*, it's nothing like you'd hoped or dreamed?

Maybe you, too, know deep down in your soul you were created to make a difference in the world, but it seems like every time you turn around, "life happens." Now you feel so beat up you're afraid even to try. What if you choose the wrong path? You might run out of money, ability, or time. No one has time to waste.

What if I told you I could show you how to find the answers to all those questions? What if I could show you how to overcome your insecurities so you're no longer afraid to explore new possibilities? I want to introduce you to a world where you no longer feel the need to compare your accomplishments to those of your friends or coworkers—a place where you can get confirmation and know when you're headed in the right direction.

I truly believe if you follow the path outlined in this book, God will open doors of opportunity you never dreamed possible, and others will look at you and ask how they, too, can lead a life similar to yours.

Does that sound interesting? Below is a brief synopsis of each of the five sections of my book, *Hey God, Do You Validate? Discover Your Purpose. Develop Your Plan. Double Your Talents.*

In Part One, *Felonies to Funerals,* I share my personal story. Inspired by my father, best-selling authors, and even God himself, I was sailing along on what I thought was the proper course for my life. But, after years of personal and professional accomplishments, I suddenly found myself financially broke and emotionally broken. One morning, I cried out to God for answers, and in the famous words of Forest Gump, "God showed up." He led me to three stories told by Jesus over 2,000 years ago. I studied these parables for months until months became years. I had lost almost everything—including my life. But that was the price I had to pay for understanding.

In Part Two, *Aptitude to Astronauts,* we look at why God created humankind—more specifically, why He made us the way we are. If you believe in God as the creator of the universe, then chances are you also believe He created you for a reason, and therefore your life has purpose. Our world praises physical, mental, and creative talents, but God is more concerned about what's happening inside our hearts. In this section, you'll gain a deeper understanding of your "God-given talents" and how to receive the affirmation we all so deeply crave.

In Part Three, *Purpose to Passion,* I'll share the "meaning of life." I'm not kidding. God has a special plan for your life. After all, you were uniquely created to carry it out. But it's essential to understand that *His plan* is not the same thing as *our purpose.* A plan is merely a course of action designed to achieve a desired result. Sometimes, unfortunately, we become passionate about the wrong things, making it impossible to achieve our goals. In this section, you'll come to understand the importance and potential dangers of passions. It only stands to reason that we should strive to become great at fulfilling our purpose in life. But to become great requires passion and passion involves emotions that can be hard to contain.

In Part Four, *Fear to Faithfulness,* we take a hard look at, you guessed it, fear and faith. Outwardly, almost everyone is afraid of something: snakes, public speaking, heights, etc. But more common fears are things like loneliness, failure, rejection, and change. In this section, we take a deep dive into the backbone of this book—a Bible story called The Parable of the Talents. In the story, there are three servants who represent me, you, and the rest of humanity. God's unique plan for each day of our lives is rooted in our unique abilities, strengths, and giftings. However, having faith that God has given us what is needed to "double our talents" is in constant competition with the fear that we don't have what it takes to get the job done.

In Part Five, *Gong Show to Talent Show,* we discuss applying what we've learned in the previous sections—what to expect, when to say no, and when to move on. William Shakespeare wrote, "All the world's a stage, and all the men and women merely players..." We are all in one big talent show, longing for a standing ovation. But all too often, we are playing to the wrong audience. It's important to know what's important, and in this section, we take a hard look into our past so we can live an abundant life in the future. The objective is simple—we want to hear God say, "Well done."

I spent years twisting the Bible to fit a narrative that made me feel like I was somehow better than everyone else. But after years of desperation and more failures than I care to count, I finally understood what God had been trying to tell me all along. It gave me hope, and for the first time in a very long time, I found peace. That's my desire for you as well. But I also want you to understand why it's essential to live a life of passion and purpose intentionally.

Here are some things you can expect to gain by reading this book...

- Discover God's unique plan and overall purpose for your life
- Understand why God's plan for your life is too important to ignore
- Learn the significance of "doubling your talents"
- Regain a sense of purpose, direction, and focus
- Find unexpected and undeserved opportunities
- Embrace new opportunities with enthusiasm
- Learn why overcoming self-doubt is easier than you think
- Increase the level of joy and satisfaction in your life today
- Build a legacy that impacts future generations
- Receive the affirmation, approval, respect, and honor you've been longing for

I realize that's a pretty lofty list of claims, and maybe you find it hard to believe you could gain so much by simply reading a book. But even if you only accomplished two or three items listed above, how much better would your life be? More importantly, on the opposite end of the spectrum are the things listed below that might come to pass if you don't embrace the principles in this book...

- Continue to live with crippling insecurities, fear, and self-doubt
- Watch as less talented people take advantage of opportunities meant for you
- Live each day with feelings of guilt and resentment
- Negatively impact your relationships at work and home
- Risk separation from the presence of God in your life

That second list describes my life not so long ago, and that's not the entire list. I purposely left out a lot of it. But it's all there in Part I of this book—the section where I share my personal story.

So what do you think? Are you game? Are you ready to be the patriarch or matriarch your family needs? Do you want to be a history-maker? To live your life in a way that God Himself takes notice?

Believe it or not, God is counting on you. He wants you to live a life of significance. God's got big plans, and they include you. And you know what else? Those plans are much easier to implement than you might think. I promise.

In the back of this book, I've also included resources to help you develop a game plan. If you need additional copies of the applications, you can find them on my website, https://www.KevinMcBroom.com/HeyGod.

Now, let's get started.

Matthew 25 Scriptures

I've included the 25th chapter of Matthew from the New King James Version of the Bible as a resource. These are the words of Jesus Christ. These teachings played a major role in me writing this book, and I will be referencing them from time to time, so I wanted to give you easy access to them. You can read them now or return to them later as needed, or both.

The Parable of the Ten Virgins

1   Then the kingdom of heaven shall be likened to ten virgins who took their lamps and went out to meet the bridegroom.

2   Now five of them were wise, and five were foolish.

3   Those who were foolish took their lamps and took no oil with them,

4   but the wise took oil in their vessels with their lamps.

5   But while the bridegroom was delayed, they all slumbered and slept.

6   And at midnight a cry was heard: 'Behold, the bridegroom is coming; go out to meet him!'

7   Then all those virgins arose and trimmed their lamps.

8   And the foolish said to the wise, 'Give us some of your oil, for our lamps are going out.'

9   But the wise answered, saying, 'No, lest there should not be enough for us and you; but go rather to those who sell, and buy for yourselves.'

10 And while they went to buy, the bridegroom came, and those who were ready went in with him to the wedding; and the door was shut.

11 Afterward the other virgins came also, saying, 'Lord, Lord, open to us!'

12 But he answered and said, 'Assuredly, I say to you, I do not know you.'

13 Watch, therefore, for you know neither the day nor the hour in which the Son of Man is coming.

The Parable of the Talents

14 For the kingdom of heaven is like a man traveling to a far country, who called his own servants and delivered his goods to them.

15 And to one he gave five talents, to another two, and to another one, to each according to his own ability; and immediately he went on a journey.

16 Then he who had received the five talents went and traded with them, and made another five talents.

17 And likewise, he who had received two gained two more also.

18 But he who had received one went and dug in the ground, and hid his lord's money.

19 After a long time, the lord of those servants came and settled accounts with them.

20 So he who had received five talents came and brought five other talents, saying, 'Lord, you delivered to me five talents; look, I have gained five more talents besides them.'

21 His lord said to him, 'Well done, good and faithful servant; you were faithful over a few things, I will make you ruler over many things. Enter into the joy of your lord.'

22 He also who had received two talents came and said, 'Lord, you delivered to me two talents; look, I have gained two more talents besides them.'

23 His lord said to him, 'Well done, good and faithful servant; you have been faithful over a few things, I will make you ruler over many things. Enter into the joy of your lord.'

24 Then he who had received the one talent came and said, 'Lord, I knew you to be a hard man, reaping where you have not sown, and gathering where you have not scattered seed.

25 And I was afraid, and went and hid your talent in the ground. Look, there you have what is yours.'

26 But his lord answered and said to him, 'You wicked and lazy servant, you knew that I reap where I have not sown, and gather where I have not scattered seed.

27 So you ought to have deposited my money with the bankers, and at my coming I would have received back my own with interest.

28 So take the talent from him, and give it to him who has ten talents.

29 'For to everyone who has, more will be given, and he will have abundance; but from him who does not have, even what he has will be taken away.

30 And cast the unprofitable servant into the outer darkness. There will be weeping and gnashing of teeth.'

Judgement of the Gentiles

31 When the Son of Man comes in His glory, and all the holy angels with Him, then He will sit on the throne of His glory.

32 All the nations will be gathered before Him, and He will separate them one from another, as a shepherd divides his sheep from the goats.

33 And He will set the sheep on His right hand, but the goats on the left.

34 Then the King will say to those on His right hand, 'Come, you blessed of My Father, inherit the kingdom prepared for you from the foundation of the world.

35 for I was hungry and you gave Me food; I was thirsty and you gave Me drink; I was a stranger and you took Me in;

36 I was naked and you clothed Me; I was sick and you visited Me; I was in prison and you came to Me.'

37 Then the righteous will answer Him, saying, 'Lord, when did we see You hungry and feed You, or thirsty and give You drink?

38 When did we see You a stranger and take You in, or naked and clothed You?

39 Or when did we see You sick, or in prison, and come to You?'

40 And the King will answer and say to them, 'Assuredly, I say to you, inasmuch as you did it to one of the least of these My brethren, you did it to Me.'

41 Then He will also say to those on the left hand, 'Depart from Me, you cursed, into the everlasting fire prepared for the devil and his angels:

42 for I was hungry and you gave Me no food; I was thirsty and you gave Me no drink;

43 I was a stranger and you did not take Me in, naked and you did not clothe Me, sick and in prison and you did not visit Me.'

44 Then they also will answer Him, saying, 'Lord, when did we see You hungry or thirsty or a stranger or naked or sick or in prison, and did not minister to You?'

45 Then He will answer them, saying, 'Assuredly, I say to you, inasmuch as you did not do it to one of the least of these, you did not do it to Me.'

46 And these will go away into everlasting punishment, but the righteous into eternal life.

Matthew 25:1–46 New King James Version (NKJV)

PART I
Felonies to Funerals

CHAPTER 1

I Hate Camping

We're all in one big talent show, longing for a standing ovation.

BOOOOM! There was a flash of light accompanied by an instantaneous and deafening clap of thunder. All sorts of thoughts leaped into my mind at the same time. "What was that?" "Where am I?" "Is that rain?" All my questions were answered as another bolt of lightning struck. Immediately, thunder began rumbling, like it was struggling to push through the clouds. But then, all at once, it broke through with another BOOOOM!

The lightning had allowed reality to catch up with all the thoughts racing through my mind. With that brief flash of light, I saw that my oldest son, Andrew, was still asleep in his sleeping bag (nothing could wake up my ten-year-old), and I was on my brand-new cot inside our brand-new tent.

"I hate camping," I said out loud. But it didn't matter because there was no way any of the other fathers on this scouting trip could hear me over the pouring rain. I didn't know if it was midnight or almost dawn. I had left my flip phone in the truck, my only source of telling time. I assumed the storm must be moving quickly because the thunder was delayed several additional seconds after each new lightning strike. I was relieved because, honestly, it scared the living snot out of me. I don't think I've ever heard anything as loud as those two claps of thunder.

The lightning allowed me to play a "red light, green light" game until I found my flashlight inside a tent pocket. I clicked it on. Everything seemed secure, and Andrew was still out cold. So I laid back down and tried, unsuccessfully, to sleep for what seemed like two or three hours.

At some point, however, I must have dozed off because I woke to the uncourteous conversations of the scouting professionals. You know who I'm talking about. You've seen them. They look like postmen in their tall green socks, bandanas secured with a boa, and pressed uniforms covered with distinguished badges of honor for things like pooping in a bucket.

I think I was meant to have daughters. I'm better suited to hang out with the few brave-hearted moms who, hours after dawn, appear from their tents in baggy sweatpants, their husband's jackets swallowing them whole while sporting hairdos that are more like *hair-don'ts*, if you know what I mean. They stumble around the campsite in a half-awake stupor, following the scent of coffee. Maybe that's why it's called "roughing it." Anyway, back to my story.

I bounced up and down on my squeaky cot, turning my body over in jerking motions to ensure that I didn't tip over onto the floor. It was barely light outside. But I had no problem making out the image of my poor, shivering Andrew lying in a fetal position in two inches of water. He was still asleep and trying to stay warm in his brand-new, soaking-wet sleeping bag.

I carried my cot and a few other items that were still dry to my truck. After putting Andrew in the front seat and covering him with my sleeping bag, I marched over to the professionals. I interrupted their steak-and-eggs breakfast when I announced, "Hey guys, there's a brand-new tent and sleeping bag over there if anybody wants it. We'll pick up Andrew's camping badge Thursday night at the next meeting." As my dad used to say, "We didn't say goodbye, kiss my grits, ner nothin'." I defiantly hopped into my truck, and we headed to the house.

Only twelve hours earlier, around six o'clock the evening before our morning exodus, I was trying hard to make a go of it. We arrived in the early afternoon. I began to act like I knew what I was doing as I unboxed my new tent and tried to figure out where all the stinking fiberglass poles were supposed to go without reading the instructions. Even harder than setting the tent up was trying to convince Andrew that he should be helping me rather than running off into the woods to play with his friends.

After setting up our campsite and eating Lunchables for dinner, I thought to myself, for a moment, that this mini-adventure might be worthwhile. After all, according to my wife, I work too much and need to spend more quality time with our sons. So I took a deep breath and prepared myself for mindless chitchat while sizing up all the strangers standing around the campfire. "Not him...no...no...oh heavens, no. Hey, wait. I think I've met him before. His son, Seth, was in my wife's fifth-grade class last year. What was his name?"

CHAPTER 2

The Demerit

They say if you want to learn something, you should try teaching it to a middle schooler. I don't know who "they" are, but "they're" right.

Demerit. Now, there's a word you've not heard since your days in military school. My wife, Pam, has spent most of her career teaching middle school history, 5th through 8th grade, in private Christian schools. It was an enormous blessing for us as parents, allowing our sons to get their education in a private school setting. I'm a small businessman, so I'm always strapped for cash. There's no way I would have paid for my kids to go to school without the discount we received from Pam working there.

Being an educator, Pam has always taken on the overseer's role for our boys' school involvement, with one exception—discipline. So, when our oldest received a demerit, I was called in for active duty.

Demerit is essentially the opposite of merit for those unfamiliar with the terminology. If you merit a person's actions, you reward or honor them. For instance, a teacher might give a student a gold star to celebrate her learning accomplishments. A demerit would be the *opposite* of receiving a gold star. Our sons' school used a demerit system to keep students in line. The system had what we have coined today as a "three strikes, and you're out" policy. A child receiving three warnings in one week would receive a demerit. So, in other words, a student could receive two warnings without being punished.

It was a Tuesday night. I came home from work, and Pam informed me that Andrew had already received a demerit only two days into the week, and he had a form I needed to sign acknowledging I was aware he was being punished.

"I called to him, "Andrew, come in here, and let's talk about what's been going on at school."

On his way into the living room, Andrew yelled, "It's not fair!"

"Andrew," I said, "Today is Tuesday. So I'm going to go out on a limb and guess that you received both the first and second warnings on Monday, yesterday, and probably by the same teacher. Am I right?"

He confirmed, "Yeah, but..."

I interrupted and had him share how he got the first two warnings.

Andrew explained how he had gotten the first warning on Monday for cutting up in class. He was upset about getting reprimanded, so he lashed out at his teacher in front of his classmates, which made his teacher angry enough to issue a second warning within minutes of the first.

"So, what part do you think is unfair, Andrew?" I asked.

He then told me the rest of the story. He and his friend, Seth, were cutting up in class. According to Andrew, his teacher knew both boys were guilty but only warned Andrew. Andrew whined, "Seth was doing it too, but he didn't get in trouble because he's got ADHD and takes medicine for it."

"Andrew," I said, "I want to try to explain something to you. Do you remember that camping trip we were on a couple of years ago when we woke up, and our tent was full of water?"

"Yes, sir. How could I forget?"

"Well, Seth and his dad were on that camping trip, too, and I spent some time talking to Seth's dad the night before the storm. I tried to tell his dad about a book called *Rich Dad, Poor Dad.*"

"Yeah," Andrew nodded. "I've heard you talk about it."

"I explained to Seth's dad how, in this book, he could learn to make investments that would protect him in case he ever lost his job. But no matter how much I encouraged him to read the book, he kept coming up with reasons why it wouldn't work for him. For example, he said he couldn't quit his job because they needed health insurance. But when I explained he didn't need to quit his job, he pushed back again and said working on things outside of his job might get him fired. No matter what I said, he always came up with another excuse."

I could see that I was starting to lose Andrew, so I got to the point. "I think I know why your teacher didn't punish Seth, and it's not because he's on medication."

Then I shared with Andrew the story of The Parable of the Talents from the Bible. (We'll look at this parable in several of the upcoming chapters of this book, so don't panic if the references are a little confusing for you at this point). "So you see, Andrew, God expects us to be like the five-talent servant and double the things he gives us. Are you following what I'm getting at?"

Andrew shrugged.

"Look, buddy," I continued, "I know Seth's parents. They're average folks who are satisfied with where they're at today. Don't get me wrong; his parents are great people. They love each other and their kids, seem to be good Christians, and are active in their church. But they are one-talent people." I paused to see if he was following my point, but he wasn't.

"So, what's that got to do with Seth not getting a demerit?"

I thought hard before answering, "If Seth's dad is satisfied with where he is today, and he's not interested in becoming the best he can be in life, then chances are, neither is Seth. There's a saying that the apple doesn't fall far from the tree. That means that..." I abruptly stopped. Even though this made perfect sense to me, I could see Andrew was still struggling to follow. I regrouped.

"Look, Andrew. I'd be willing to bet that Seth is just like his dad—he isn't interested in becoming a part of something important in life. He's afraid of what it takes to be great in life, and your teacher knows that. She also knows you have what it takes to be a five-talent man, and when you were cutting up with Seth in class, you were wasting your talents. That's why she gave you a demerit." I hoped Andrew understood my point because I was pretty impressed with what was coming out of my mouth.

They say that if you want to learn something, you should try teaching it to middle schoolers. I don't know who *they* are, but *they're* right. I had just uncovered something that would perplex my mind and tear at the very fabric of my soul for the next decade. You see, I was already living a life full of impressive accomplishments. But with those accomplishments came an insatiable ego. The hard truth was the praises of others meant more to me than the actual achievements themselves.

I had left that scouting trip two years earlier, thinking it had been a complete waste of time and money. Today, however, I can see the divine appointment that evening by the campfire, in the calm before the storm.

By the way, I still hate camping.

CHAPTER 3

The Book I Didn't Read That Changed My Life

Writing down your goals is like buying a ticket to a better life.

Bob stood in the parking lot in front of his modest pizza restaurant. He watched as two tall, youthful gentlemen leaned ladders against the building and began installing a new sign on the business beside his. Bob walked up to a guy named Steve, who appeared to be in charge, and asked him, "You like my sign?"

Steve Martin, not the one you are thinking of, was the owner of Martin Signs. Even though he had yet to reach the age of thirty, he had been painting signs for nearly a decade, starting his career at Coca-Cola back in the days when Coke gave a sign to almost any business located on a well-traveled road.

Steve changed his focus for a moment to look at Bob's sign. It was a lighted box sign with a picture of a guy who looked like he knew how to make pizza, complete with a handlebar mustache and a chef's hat. Bold letters spelled out "Hungry Herman's."

"Sure, it looks nice," Steve said while probably wondering why this guy was keeping him from his work.

Bob enlightened him, "My friend painted that sign. He's about to finish college and looking for a job. You ought to hire him." Bob's not one to beat around the bush.

That was in May of 1988. The same month that I got my business degree from Tennessee Tech University. For me, the '80s was a decade of one milestone after another—some noteworthy and some I'd rather forget.

I graduated from high school in 1983 and met Pam the following fall on my first day of college. We went on our first date the following evening, and that night, I told a mutual friend, "I just went on a date with the girl I'm going to marry." I've said it many times and sincerely mean it when I say that the only good thing I got out of college was my wife, and I met her on the very first day. I should have quit while I was ahead.

College was an opportunity for me to spread my entrepreneurial wings for the first time. My drugs of choice, marijuana, and cocaine, became both my business and my pleasure. As with most people who go down this path, it caught up with me, and in the latter part of 1986, I was arrested on multiple felony drug charges. I was facing a maximum sentence of something like 75 years in prison. Fortunately, that was enough to snap my 21-year-old butt into reality.

It wasn't as easy as flipping a switch, but with my family's support and a renewed relationship with God, I got pointed in the right direction. Pam and I married in August 1987, about five months before my sentencing. Most of my charges had either been dropped or reduced, but my attorney told me I should expect to receive a 12-year prison sentence, meaning I'd get out in about four or five years with good behavior.

The legal proceedings at my sentencing were surreal because I expected to go straight from the courtroom to the state prison. After being on the stand for what seemed like an eternity, the judge looked over at me and said, "Well, son, do you have anything you'd like to add before I hand down your sentence?"

I can't remember if I knew I would get an opportunity to speak on my own behalf, but I distinctly remember how ready I was for all of the uncertainty to be over, so I shared my heart.

"Your honor, I've broken the law. I knew what I was doing was wrong, and I have no excuses. I'm prepared to accept whatever sentence you think is best." I said it, and I meant it. Nevertheless, somehow, I knew that God's plan for my life didn't include me going to prison.

The judge looked at me over the top of his reading glasses, spoke a few words of chastisement, and then announced my sentence—one year of in-house arrest and five years of probation. This meant I could only go to work, school, and church, and I would have to wear an ankle bracelet tracking my whereabouts, but I wouldn't be going to prison. Essentially, I had just been given a second chance on the next five years of my life.

Had I gone to prison, I doubt I would have ever finished college. I want to think that my marriage could have withstood my being away from Pam for several years, but who knows? I wouldn't have painted the Hungry Herman's sign for my best friend, Bob, and I wouldn't have had the opportunity to work at Martin Signs. By the way, today, Pam and I own Martin Signs.

When Steve Martin offered me a job to run his company in the summer of 1988, I accepted with the condition that I would only commit to one year. Honestly, I wasn't too excited about working for someone else. Nor was I excited about making signs. But I needed someone to give me a break—an opportunity to prove myself.

When the year was up, Steve offered me 50% of his company if I would agree to stay and work with him. The thought of being a partner in a business at the age of 24 was honoring. But Pam and I had received another offer we just couldn't pass up. So we decided to head out west for an adventure of a lifetime.

As I said before, the 1980s was a decade of milestones for me. The same was true for my father. Dad was a former army helicopter pilot, but he had always had a knack for business. In the early '80s, he had aggressively built a home healthcare company with multiple locations. However, through a series of miscalculations, my father found himself owing six figures in back taxes. He subsequently lost everything and filed for bankruptcy.

So, what do you do when you think you can conquer the world but don't have a pot to pee in? Well, if you're my dad, you move to the most expensive city in America—Aspen, Colorado. I'm completely serious. That's what he did. And apparently, he found some folks more desperate than him because he was able to buy a grocery store in the Aspen Airport Business Center and a house in the nearby town of Basalt. Keep in mind that he was flat broke.

Now, all of this happened about one year before I started working at Martin Signs. It didn't take long before my father got antsy to get back into the home healthcare business and began courting Pam and me to move to Aspen to run the grocery store. This is where we come back to the part of my story where I turned down Steve Martin's offer to become a partner in his company. But more importantly, this is where we come to the point of this chapter where I tell you about the book I never read that changed the direction of my young life.

One evening, while Pam and I were at our *tiny* apartment just down the street from my father's house in Basalt, he paid us a visit. He said he wanted to help me "Get some motivation in life." I was a typical twenty-something-year-old with no direction. My main goal was to find more time to enjoy Colorado—skiing, golfing, and exploring the Rocky Mountains with my wife.

Dad told me he had just read a book called *The Magic of Thinking Big* by David Schwartz. He learned about the book while watching an interview with Lou Holtz, the head football coach at Notre Dame. The book inspired Holtz, and apparently my dad, to make a list of audacious goals. Holtz had 107 goals on his list and had already accomplished 80 of them within 20 years. According to his internet blog, as of today, he has completed 102 so far. Now that's impressive.

Dad didn't buy me the book or tell me to read it. Instead, he said, "I want you to get a piece of paper and a pen and write down all the things you would want to accomplish in life if money, time, ability, and support were not obstacles." He told me I should come up with 100 things.

I struggled. I sat there on the shag carpet by our wood-burning stove for about an hour and could only come up with twenty-one goals. Most were simple and attainable, although, at the time, most felt like they were entirely out of reach. Things like having a son, owning a house, owning a business, and going on a cruise. These seemed logical and doable in time. But still, they were unimaginable to me at that point in my life. Next were things I hadn't thought of before, but they felt right, like learning to play the piano and speaking a second language. I even had a few stupid ones, like skydiving and performing in front of a twelve-piece orchestra.

I tucked the list away and didn't think about it much for several years. I would recall items on my list from time to time as I achieved one, like when we bought our first home two years later or when we got to go on a company cruise the following year. I thought it would have been at least ten years before either happened.

Then, one day, about five years after making the list, I ran across it while moving. I sat down and pored over it in complete disbelief. Out of the twenty-one goals I wrote down, I accomplished seventeen. It would be another ten years before I would jump out of an airplane—leaving only three items on my original list. I still can't speak a second language, and I'm not much of a piano player—which may explain why I haven't performed with a twelve-piece orchestra. However, eighty-five percent of the items I wrote down had been accomplished in under five years.

I would have never guessed that there was some sort of magic in *thinking big* and writing down goals, but there really is. I once heard Brian Tracy, a motivational speaker, say that less than 3% of people have written goals, and only about 1% review them regularly. I can't explain it, but it makes a difference. Writing down your goals is like buying a ticket to a better life.

I used to say, "I wish my dad would teach me something on purpose because I only got to learn from his mistakes." But my dad did teach me something on purpose. He taught me the importance of writing down goals by introducing me to "The Magic of Thinking Big." Honestly, until I began writing this book, I had forgotten I had my dad to thank for how I became so passionate about goal setting.

Isn't it funny how a book I never read impacted my life so profoundly? But two other books have influenced me even more; *Rich Dad, Poor Dad,* and *The Bible*—maybe because I've read them.

CHAPTER 4

—

Poor Dad

*Every time I proudly proclaim, "I'll never do that again,"
life serves up a healthy helping of humble pie.*

Aspen, Colorado, was unlike any city I had ever witnessed. It seemed to be a magnet for stupid-wealthy people who wanted to be seen and stupid-broke people hoping to hang out with the stupid-wealthy. It was a treasure trove of trust fund babies who spent their time partying, skiing, and looking for a cause to fight for. Vegetarian rights for dogs and fur bans were in vogue when we lived there in the late '80s.

Pam and I weren't partiers, and we worked too much to ski. But we loved the adventurous lifestyle we experienced high in the Rocky Mountains. As crazy as this may sound, we had only been there for two years when my father announced that the lease on our grocery store wouldn't be renewed. Everything I had busted my butt to help build at The Aspen Grocery was gone within a month. We stood by helplessly and watched as the building and business were literally bulldozed to the ground.

My dad quickly shifted gears and began fast-tracking his home healthcare management company while keeping me busy doing the bookkeeping. A few months later, we moved the business to Park City, Utah, to be closer to an actual city with a real airport and, hopefully, real people.

Pam and I thrived in Park City and became regular, middle-class people for the first time. I worked a typical number of hours compared to my usual 60 or 70-hour workweek in Aspen. Pam got a teaching job, and we bought our first home—a little condo about five miles from town. We now had time for friends and got heavily involved in church. In January 1993, we celebrated the arrival of our first son, Andrew.

Dad's new business experienced faster growth than I could have ever imagined. Within two years, we had employees and interests all over the United States. He even bought a travel agency to "save money" because we were traveling so much. I was being pulled in a dozen different directions, yet I was having the time of my life. Soon, however, I began to suspect my dad was hiding things from me. It seemed like every time I walked into his office, conversations would end awkwardly. The more I tried to corner him, the more I was assigned to projects out of town.

In the summer of 1993, while speaking to a group of nurses in Wyoming, I was informed I had an emergency call. I asked everyone to excuse me for a moment but never returned. Our secretary was on the phone, "Kevin, the FBI is here. They're confiscating all our file cabinets and going through your and your dad's offices. Nobody can find your dad. Oh, and there's a TV news truck outside. I'm not kidding. What do you want me to do?"

I jumped in my company vehicle and started the drive home. I tracked down my dad before I got back to Utah. He asked me to break into his house, empty his safe, load up my family, and drive to Oregon, where he had rented a place for us to stay.

Once we got settled in, Dad confessed everything. He cried so hard he could barely speak. It turns out he had never paid his back taxes from almost ten years earlier, and he had been paying his mom out of his company. His mom wasn't an employee; she was a client, and my father's company managed her healthcare business.

At first, I didn't understand why the FBI was involved. But that was before he explained to us how the payments to his mom could be considered kickbacks and Medicare fraud. To make matters worse, the government would most likely assume I was also involved.

Dad wanted us to stay in Oregon for a week, but Pam and I packed up and left for Utah after just one day. I wasn't feeling very sympathetic, and this was certainly no time for a vacation. Dad was right. The FBI did think I was involved. He had told me I should hire a lawyer to accompany me to the FBI interviews, but that was easier said than done. I no longer had a job, and Pam and I had zero savings. I certainly didn't have money for a lawyer, and besides, why should I need one if I hadn't done anything wrong?

It took some time, but the Feds eventually realized I wasn't hiding anything. Honestly, all they had to do was look at my very modest home and empty bank account to realize that I wasn't profiting from whatever my dad was into. Heck, I didn't even own a car. I had always been upset about how little my dad was paying me while he was making millions by all appearances. But, in the end, I guess that's what convinced the Feds that I wasn't personally involved in anything illegal.

It was apparent my dad was about to go to prison. Pam and I quickly realized that even though we loved being out west, we needed to do what was best for our six-month-old son. Ironically, the day before the FBI showed up at our office, Pam told my stepmother, "I'll never live in Tennessee again." But within two weeks after speaking those words, we had sold everything that wouldn't fit into a U-haul truck, and we were on our way back to the support we knew we'd find from family and friends in Cookeville.

We moved into a small apartment owned by my grandfather, borrowed a car from my mom, and lived as frugally as possible until our condo in Utah was sold a few months later. Steve was no longer willing to give me half his sign company, but that didn't matter. The proceeds from the sale of our home gave me enough money to become his partner and accomplish another item on my list of goals—I was a business owner.

CHAPTER 5

—

Rich Dad

*It doesn't matter if you're making good time
if you don't know where you're headed.*

While settling into my new career, I started listening to a Nashville radio program with hosts Dave Ramsey and Larry Burkett. The show and books they recommended taught me a great deal about managing finances. It also introduced me to the second of the three books that have greatly influenced my life, *Rich Dad Poor Dad,* by Robert Kiyosaki.

Let me share a funny story with you. The first home we bought in Tennessee had a nice, big backyard. A chainlink fence surrounded the yard, and weeds liked to weave themselves into the fence. One fall, I decided to pull the weeds out of the fence, but it was surprisingly hard to get them untangled. So, I devised a plan to burn the weeds. I had some gasoline for my lawnmower that I knew I shouldn't let sit around all winter, and gas burns, right? So, I poured a small amount of the gas along the perimeter of the fence row and tried to set it on fire.

Now, I was cautious at first. I lit a paper towel tied to a broom handle and pushed it into the gasoline-soaked weeds—nothing. I made several attempts, each time getting a little bolder, but I could only get the fire going one little clump of weeds at a time before it went out. So, I gave up on my original plan, and instead, I created an "Indiana Jones" torch and walked over to start systematically burning the weeds one section at a time.

You probably know where this is going, so I'll go ahead and tell you that I didn't get hurt—other than losing my eyebrows. I was slowly burning the weeds when suddenly, I heard a series of whooshing sounds, growing faster and louder. The next thing I knew, I was lying flat on my back, unable to breathe because the fire had robbed all the oxygen from the air. There was a blinding amount of smoke for probably five or ten minutes, and we lived a couple of houses down from a busy intersection. The smoke was so thick people couldn't see to drive. The fire went out almost as fast as it started, but regardless, a fire truck showed up a few minutes later. Like a little kid, I ran inside and acted like I didn't know what had happened.

I tell you this story not only because it's funny but to emphasize the point that reading *Rich Dad Poor Dad* was like pouring gasoline on my financial goals. I became obsessed with building passive income streams, and each accomplishment came faster and was more significant than the one before it—*Whoosh*. Unlike *The Magic of Thinking Big*, I've read *Rich Dad Poor Dad*. In fact, I've read it at least twenty times. I've also read the dozen or so other books Kiyosaki has done as follow-ups.

In *Rich Dad Poor Dad*, Kiyosaki emphasizes the principle of acquiring investments like securities, businesses, and real estate that pay out passive income—meaning you don't actually work for the income. It's like an interest-bearing savings account—the bank pays you interest even though you haven't worked to earn it. Your money does the work for you. By putting this into practice, you can slowly build a passive income stream, giving you financial security if you someday find yourself unable to work.

My grandfather was a real estate investor, so it was only natural for me to choose real estate as the primary vehicle to achieve my financial goals. He became my mentor and even allowed me to partner with him on some residential and commercial investments.

As I said earlier, I became obsessed with building passive income streams. I felt like I had discovered a hidden secret to success, so I wanted to share it. I told everyone what I was doing. But, unfortunately, most were like Seth's dad, whom I introduced in Chapter 2. They feared the unknown and probably thought I was trying to sign them up for a multilevel marketing program.

Most people instinctively run from fear. But during that part of my life, I had zero fear of failing. So, during that season of blind ambition, I acquired about twenty rental properties, 100% ownership of Martin Signs, 50% ownership in a competing sign company, as well as a stupid, expensive retail furniture company. I also got my general contractor's license and started building two or three spec homes yearly. Looking back, it's hard to believe I could juggle everything I had going on.

I once heard a young man in my Sunday school class share a revelation he had while doing pushups on his living room rug. After completing all he could, he lay on his chest, resting with his nose a few inches away from the floor. He had walked over that rug hundreds of times. But, as he lay there, it struck him that he couldn't remember what the rug looked like. He could only make out a maze-like pattern in his peripheral view. *I don't remember this design being a part of my rug,* he thought. Then, he stood up and was amazed to see the same pattern repeated over and over. While he was resting, he had been so close that he couldn't see how the pattern fit into the bigger picture of the overall design.

He shared how, in a way, the discovery about his rug paralleled his life; he was so close to what he was involved in each day that he couldn't see the significance of how it impacted his overall life. But when he examined a seemingly unimportant event from five years earlier, he could recognize the significance and how it helped determine his present-day life.

That's where I was—the proverbial "Couldn't see the forest for the trees." I was focusing most of my time on one area, my financial goals, so my achievements were monumental and numerous. Yet, all the while, I was neglecting my relationships, health, and even my walk with God. Goals like praying with my wife, reading the Bible, exercising, community involvement, and developing leadership skills suffered or didn't make the list at all.

Today, I can easily see how much I missed the mark. But the *Rich Dad Poor Dad* book wasn't the only source for my misguided understanding of my purpose in life. You see, I also felt like I had received confirmation from another book—my favorite Book. And it wasn't merely a confirmation; it was a mandate from God himself, or so I thought.

CHAPTER 6

——

My Favorite Story

You can fool some of the people some of the time.
But, you're a fool if you think you can fool God.

Jesus Christ, the son of God, taught the people using stories we call *parables*. Parables are like the ultimate form of a simile. Even though they often reference terminology and traditions from 2000 years ago, the lessons still apply to life today, and they always will. The storylines are timeless.

Located before the first chapter of this book, you'll find the entire 25th chapter of Matthew from the New Testament of the Bible. It will give you a handy place to access it for reference as you work your way through this book. But for our purposes right now, I'd like you to read The Parable of the Talents found in Matthew 25:14-30 before continuing with this chapter—so here it is.

• • •

14 For the kingdom of heaven is like a man traveling to a far country, who called his own servants and delivered his goods to them.

15 And to one he gave five talents, to another two, and to another one, to each according to his own ability; and immediately he went on a journey.

16 Then he who had received the five talents went and traded with them and made another five talents.

17 And likewise he who had received two gained two more also.

18 But he who had received one went and dug in the ground, and hid his lord's money.

19 After a long time the lord of those servants came and settled accounts with them.

20 So he who had received five talents came and brought five other talents, saying, 'Lord, you delivered to me five talents; look, I have gained five more talents besides them.'

21 His lord said to him, 'Well done, good and faithful servant; you were faithful over a few things, I will make you ruler over many things. Enter into the joy of your lord.'

22 He also who had received two talents came and said, 'Lord, you delivered to me two talents; look, I have gained two more talents besides them.'

23 His lord said to him, 'Well done, good and faithful servant; you have been faithful over a few things, I will make you ruler over many things. Enter into the joy of your lord.'

24 Then he who had received the one talent came and said, 'Lord, I knew you to be a hard man, reaping where you have not sown, and gathering where you have not scattered seed.

25 And I was afraid, and went and hid your talent in the ground. Look, there you have what is yours.'

26 But his lord answered and said to him, 'You wicked and lazy servant, you knew that I reap where I have not sown, and gather where I have not scattered seed.

27 So you ought to have deposited my money with the bankers, and at my coming I would have received back my own with interest.

28 Therefore take the talent from him, and give it to him who has ten talents.

29 'For to everyone who has, more will be given, and he will have abundance; but from him who does not have, even what he has will be taken away.

30 And cast the unprofitable servant into the outer darkness. There will be weeping and gnashing of teeth.'

Matthew 25:14-30 New King James Version (NKJV)

• • •

At first glance, you may look at this parable and think like I did. The Bible says that where your treasure lies, there your heart will also be. My "treasure" was in building wealth, and because that's where my heart was, that's the message I got from this parable. But, I didn't look at it in context with the scriptures preceding and following it, nor did I take the time to try and understand what God was really saying.

We've all heard the saying about somebody who only hears what they want to hear. Well, that was me. The only thing I wanted to hear was that I was on the right track, and as far as I was concerned, I'd just gotten my confirmation from the *Big Man upstairs* Himself.

If you are new to the scriptures or unfamiliar with this story, let me clarify things. In the parable, the lord, or master, is Jesus, and it's safe to assume we are currently living in what is referenced as His journey to a faraway country. Christians, or believers, as Christians tend to call themselves, are represented by the three servants.

The translation of the scriptures above comes from the New King James Version, which uses the word *talent* to describe the goods the master gave his servants. Other translations of the Bible substitute the word talents with "bags of silver or gold," and some even use the word "land" or "property." For me, any of these translations worked because I was trying to follow the teachings of *Rich Dad Poor Dad*, which is all about financial growth.

And this brings us back full circle to when Andrew got his demerit, and I told him about The Parable of the Talents. I was trying to teach something to my son, but all I ended up doing was bragging about my own goals and accomplishments.

I was proud of my financial and business achievements. They made me feel important, and I received praise from friends, family, and even strangers with each newly completed venture. These accolades fueled my pride and filled the void of my father's constant reminder that I didn't measure up. "Try to be something," he'd always tell me. And so, I tried to become what I thought my earthly father wanted me to be.

I wish I could say I woke up one morning and said, "Hey, wait a minute. I think I'm missing something here." That would've been so much easier. But that's not what happened. Blinded by my pride, I was about to walk smack dab face-first into a seven-year stretch of unimaginable trials, pain, and suffering.

CHAPTER 7

———

Lost in America

Sometimes, I think God forgets to wind his watch.

My oldest son, Andrew, struggled with direction in his first year of college. After less than stellar academic success and some personal setbacks, he sent his mother and me a letter saying he needed to take some time off from school to "find himself." I must admit, at the time, I found the statement pretty comical. Ironically, a couple of years later, if you'd asked me what word best described my place in life, I would have said *lost*.

I was at the height of my business success. I could hardly believe the growth of our sign company and other business ventures. However, like most young businesses, we were walking a financial tightrope. The early 2000s, or as I like to call them, "the naughts," were a time of loose lending by the banks. As a financial risk-taker, it felt like a safety net to me, and so I took advantage of almost every opportunity that came my way. But in 2007, the housing bubble popped and ushered in what we now call the "Great Recession."

Pam and I most likely would have come out of the economic downturn unscathed had I not decided to buy a retail furniture store in February of 2007. As it turned out, it was one of the worst times in history to purchase commercial real estate, and with the housing market about to implode, it was a horrific time to get into the retail furniture business. By the time 2008 rolled around, I knew we were in trouble.

I started taking steps to "stop the bleeding," as my dad used to call it whenever a business was hemorrhaging money. This new investment made up almost half of our overall debt, so I began focusing most of my time on the operations of the furniture store in hopes of salvaging things. Nevertheless, month-over-month sales dropped fifty percent within a year, and with real estate values plummeting, the bank ordered an appraisal of the property and building that housed the furniture store.

When we purchased the real estate in early 2007, the property appraised at $1,100,000. But within two years, the value dropped to $757,000, and as the recession wained on, the bank ordered yet another appraisal in late 2010—$450,000. The furniture store was losing thousands of dollars every month. We knew it was only a matter of time before the bank would step in. Of course, they were hoping the economy would turn around as much as we were. I kept thinking, "Maybe things will get better next quarter." But they never did.

Our sign companies were also struggling, and sales dropped about forty percent over two years. It's hard to know how much blame can be placed on the recession, but my divided focus certainly didn't help matters. I worried about our employees— some had been with me for over ten years. I worried about the local vendors and how it might affect my reputation if I couldn't pay them what we owed. It got so bad Pam and I hired an attorney to give us advice on how to avoid filing for bankruptcy.

As I look at the last few paragraphs, it sounds so mechanical and emotionless, but my life was actually falling apart. I was so overwhelmed I literally considered suicide as one of my options. I tried to hide my anxieties from our employees and stay positive at work. But most days, I failed miserably.

At home, it was even more challenging. I hated myself for putting my family through something like this, and even though I wasn't angry at them, I focused a lot of my frustrations on Pam and our boys. I didn't see how things could get any worse, but then our oldest son got kicked out of high school for an entire year. I wanted to fix the situation because that's what dads are supposed to do. But I couldn't.

I felt helpless. Life at home was horrible, and from where I stood, I was the problem. For the first time in our twenty years of marriage, I told Pam I was ready to call it quits. Fortunately, she refused to let me leave when I tried to move out. She probably saved my life.

I couldn't understand why this was happening. Where had I gotten off course? I was doing what God had instructed me to do—I was doubling my talents.

I needed some advice, so I went fishing with our pastor in hopes of hearing some words of wisdom. We were together for hours. I went on and on about how mad I was at my wife and how disappointed I was in myself. I wanted to beat the kids and kick the dog (that's supposed to be funny, by the way). My pastor only had one thing to say. "Kevin, I think you've lost your faith."

I'm thinking, "That's it? I talk non-stop for hours, and that's all you've got to say?" But, you know what? He was right. I *had* lost my faith. I was carrying out what I thought He had instructed me to do in The Parable of the Talents, and now, I felt like God had abandoned me.

Creditors pressed in on all sides while Pam and I did everything possible to avoid bankruptcy. I'd not taken a paycheck in months and began selling our investment properties to make ends meet. Finally, in May of 2011, the bank took possession of the furniture store. I called my dad to share the news.

"What are you going to do with the rest of your life?" I knew what Dad was really asking me, and it wasn't just a philosophical cliche.

After losing everything, including his freedom and family, my dad managed to buy and build up a very successful auto body business in Florida. For over ten years, he had continually asked me to sell everything in Tennessee to move to Florida to help him. About once a year, he would make me a new offer. But we chose to stay in Tennessee each time because it was what we felt was best for our sons. This time, however, things were different, and Dad knew it. Andrew was about to move to Georgia to start college, and I was at that proverbial crossroads in business and life, with no idea which way to turn.

I knew a move to Florida would be risky, but something inside me longed to have a deeper relationship with my father. My heart told me I should make one more attempt. I asked Pam for input, but as usual, she told me it was my decision. She also reminded me how he had let us down twice before.

"Do you think you can trust him?"

I hated to say it out loud, but we both knew the answer. "I doubt it," I said, shaking my head.

Nevertheless, two months later, we moved to Florida. We made some adjustments at the sign companies so that I only had to spend about an hour each day overseeing things, and Pam got a teaching job at a private Christian school. We were grateful but concerned because her salary was about half of what she made in Tennessee. My salary at the body shop was also substantially less than what I'd been making from our Tennessee companies. Well, at least when I was able to take a paycheck.

At first, Dad put some serious effort into healing some of the wounds from our past. But within a couple of months, the honeymoon was over. Pam and I had given him a list of twelve demands that he agreed to before we moved. Things like allowing us to keep our Tennessee businesses, being transparent with me about the body shop finances, and even personal items like committing to spending an hour each month with our youngest son, Isaac.

Dad wholeheartedly agreed to our list but ultimately only lived up to two of the twelve items. He started pressuring me to sell our interests in Tennessee only a month in. But it was too late to back out now—we were stuck.

I'm not trying to throw my dad under the bus. I knew what I was signing up for. Relationally, he and I were doing pretty well, even though we weren't spending as much time together as I'd hoped. All of this was overshadowed, however, by my utter contempt for my new job.

For the previous twenty years, I had been in charge. Now, I was in a work environment where it felt like no one was in charge. My dad was an incredibly successful businessman, but I'd describe his management style as schizophrenic. After ten years of success and impressive growth in the auto body business, I expected to see well-defined procedures and processes guiding his team in unison. But honestly, it was more like "every man for himself."

I knew nothing about the auto body industry, so I started at the bottom, literally. I tried to bring structure to the chaos where I could, but more often than not, I was met with animosity by my coworkers. It was so bad I once had an employee threaten to beat me up in the parking lot after work. Are you kidding me? Like threatening the owner's son is going to advance your standing in the company. Every day, as I pulled my car into work, I would take a deep breath and pray the same prayer, "God, I pray that my being here today will make this business a better place. Let me be the salt and the light."

My strengths lie in leadership and administration, and because this was my father's business, I took it personally when people took advantage of the lack of organization. Well, at least in the beginning. I hate to admit it, but as time passed, I found myself like all the other employees, focusing on what was on my desk and trying to avoid the drama.

I was miserable. My health deteriorated. At times, I would get so dizzy I couldn't walk. My right eye twitched constantly. I couldn't sleep. I went to so many different doctors that Dad called me a wimp. The doctors all said the same thing; there was nothing wrong with me—it was stress. I knew what I had to do.

One afternoon, I told my dad how much I loved and appreciated him, but I couldn't subject myself to such a toxic environment any longer. I wasn't sure what I would do for work, but I knew I wouldn't be doing it with him. I was heartbroken. After one year to the day, I left my dad's body shop.

"Why did you bring me to Florida?" I asked God over and over.

We were happy with our house, church, and Pam's new teaching job. Isaac was about to start high school. Nevertheless, Pam and I wanted to return to Tennessee. The problem was we were broke. The cost of moving would most likely force us into bankruptcy, and filing bankruptcy meant closing our sign companies and employees losing their jobs. That just wasn't an option we could live with.

So I started looking for work. When our new pastor discovered I was leaving the body shop, he asked if I would consider being the church administrator. What a blessing, I thought—no more commuting. Heck, I could even walk to work if the weather was nice.

I could tell Dad felt like I'd let him down. But I felt like he had let me down as well. When I was in Tennessee, we talked by phone almost every day. I had assumed we would spend even more time together once I was in Florida. But when I was working at the body shop, we spoke *much* less, and it was always about work. Now, with our wounded egos in the way, it was awkward to talk at all. So, Dad quit calling me altogether, and I only called him about once a week.

One Saturday morning, about two months after I'd started working at the church, I got a text from Dad asking when our Sunday morning services began. Sure enough, the next day, my father walked through the doors of our little church, wearing his favorite blue Hawaiian shirt. After church, as he was leaving, we hugged long and hard, fighting back the tears.

As I watched my dad and his wife walk to their truck, I asked God, "Is this why you brought me to Florida, so my dad would start coming back to church?"

Two weeks later, I got my answer.

CHAPTER 8

———

The Call and the Calling

*Believe it or not, God is counting on you to do something
extraordinary—something only you can do.*

For the most part, I was enjoying my new role as a church administrator. Although I have to admit, it was a lot less challenging than running a business, and I was flat-out bored most of the time. They say leading people requires patience, but leading volunteers requires what Christians call *the patience of Job*. I spent more time waiting for things to happen than actually doing something.

Nevertheless, I didn't find the time to call my dad following his visit to our little church. Honestly, I guess I was hoping he'd call me. Ten days passed. It was a Thursday afternoon, and I went home for lunch, sat down, and turned on the news. My phone rang. I wrinkled up my nose when I saw one of my dad's employees was calling. "I wonder why she would be calling me," I said out loud.

"Kevin? You're not driving, are you?"

"No, I'm just sitting here eating some lunch. Why? What's up?"

"Kevin, your father has died."

I hung up the phone. I guess it was my way of making what I had just heard go away. I knew it was true, though. She would never do something like this as a joke. She called me back to ensure I was okay, and after I calmed down a bit, she gave me more details. My father had returned to town early in the morning hours. Rather than driving home about an hour away, he decided to sleep on his boat—maybe because his wife was visiting family out of state. He had apparently died in his sleep.

That was when I stopped asking God why I was supposed to be in Florida.

Things quickly went from surreal to crazy. That night, I got a call from an old friend I had worked with years earlier. She started ranting about my stepmother having my dad killed and that I needed to have an autopsy done. Apparently, she and my dad planned on getting married, and my stepmother found out about it. I didn't know what to say. The idea that my dad's wife, whom I had known for almost ten years, was somehow involved in his death seemed absurd.

I screamed into the phone, "Look, I don't know if you're looking for money or what your deal is, but my dad just died, and I don't need this right now!" And I hung up on her. I felt terrible for her. I knew she was probably telling the truth, at least the part about the marriage plans. After all, my dad had already been married four times. So, I was never surprised to find out my father was involved with another woman.

Unfortunately, I never got to apologize to my friend for being so uncaring to her that night on the phone. Eleven days later, she, too, was found dead of unknown causes. *Her* autopsy was inconclusive. My stepmother refused to perform an autopsy on my dad, and I soon learned that the law would prohibit my sisters and me from having any say in the matter. Whenever I suggested foul play to the police, they told me I'd been watching too much TV. I wasn't sure what to believe and even less sure what to do about it. It's not like you go through this sort of thing every day.

And as if that wasn't enough, my father didn't have a will. So my sisters and I found ourselves in the middle of a legal nightmare, pitting us against our step-mother and one of Dad's minority business partners. The legal battle would go on for almost three years. This whole mess had all the makings of a successful reality TV show.

Looking back, I think I was in shock following my dad's death. You'd think by this point, I would have been numb to turbulence in my life. The last handful of years had included losing businesses, Andrew being expelled from school, moving to another state, a year working the worst job ever, my dad dying, and now, a bunch of legal crap to deal with.

All this *junk* made me more grateful for my job at the church than ever before. It kept me preoccupied, and my church family went out of their way to support me. The church should have remained the one constant in my life. But even that was about to be taken from me.

I was fired from a pizza place once in college for making myself a pizza while on the clock. So, I knew what it felt like to lose a job for doing something wrong, but this was different. Our pastor asked me to join him at a restaurant for lunch, and while we ate, he rambled on for twenty minutes or so about his plans for the church and how he now realized he should have never created my position in the first place. He never actually fired me, but he clearly wanted me to step down.

Pam and I hoped we could stay on as active members at the church, but we knew it wouldn't be healthy for us to stick around. And so, just like that, I had a couple more things to add to my list of setbacks: no job and no church home.

Not working a full-time job was both a blessing and a curse. I became obsessed and spent way too much time fighting for my and my sisters' interests in our father's estate. But this newfound freedom also allowed me to spend more time pouring through my journals and questioning my past. I kept remembering when my father had asked almost two years earlier, "What are you going to do with the rest of your life?" He, of course, meant career-wise. But now, I felt like God was asking me, "Okay, Kevin, what *are* you going to do with the rest of your life?"

You've probably heard someone say that their life was off course. As I explained earlier, I could definitely relate to that expression. In fact, I'd like to tell you a parable of my own and see if it resonates with you.

• • •

The kingdom of Kevin was like a man traveling across the sea by boat. God himself had given him access to the charts for every season to ensure his headings were true. But not being a seasoned sailor, Kevin only used portions of the charts and unwittingly set a course a few degrees off. Finally, after sailing for years with the bow pointed ever so slightly off the correct heading, he made landfall—hundreds of miles south of his appointed destination.

He had been sailing, generally speaking, in the right direction, and with a strong tailwind and his sails fully trimmed, he had made good time on his journey. Nevertheless, with each passing day, he had unwittingly increased the distance and time it would take to arrive where God intended for him to land.

He could have corrected his course at any time had he only realized his miscalculation. He occasionally checked his heading to ensure he was following the correct route. But he neglected to look over all the charts at his disposal, instead relying on the single chart he used to set his original heading. He even asked others for validation, but they were also unseasoned and only marveled at his speed and progress. So, with his pride bolstered, he no longer worried about his course and enjoyed the ride.

But when he finally reached land and looked around for affirmation that he was in the right place, there was no evidence of what God had promised. And now, before he could set sail again, he had to figure out where he was and what had gone wrong.

But there was another problem. Even if Kevin knew the correct destination, he couldn't set sail because most of his supplies were gone. Restocking the ship for another journey would take some serious work and a lot of time. And so, he found himself stranded and emotionally shipwrecked.

• • •

I realize that may have been a little dramatic. But I hope the analogy helps you understand what it felt like at that moment in my life. I had gone from thinking God was validating my actions to feeling like He had abandoned me. I needed to go back to the "charts" to find my destination and determine where I had gotten off course.

God hadn't changed—He doesn't change. I knew that. But I had missed something. I had read The Parable of the Talents dozens of times—maybe hundreds. So, I started asking myself some pretty tough questions.

- What was the real meaning of talent?
- Why did each servant not have the same ability?
- Aren't we all created equal?
- Why was God angry at the servant given one talent, even though he returned the talent safely?
- Does God think I'm wicked and lazy too?
- Why didn't He give the extra talent to the servant with two talents?
- How can I know for sure what God expects of me?

These questions became the fuel to my fire. I wanted affirmation—no, I *needed* affirmation. I was determined to hear God say, "Well done, Kevin."

Please understand this "plan and purpose" I keep referring to doesn't change *everything* that goes on in my day-to-day life. I still have to put food on the table and provide for my family—that's part of God's plan for my life, too. I'm still trying to save for retirement and ensure that Pam will be cared for if I'm gone. But I now realize my financial "talents" aren't what God wants me to "double." I wish it were because that would be much easier for me.

I have another question for you. Now that you know my story, what's yours? In the next section, *Aptitude to Astronauts*, we will examine why God made us the way we are and how it should affect our values in life. Believe it or not, God is counting on you to do something extraordinary—something only you can do. He needs you to live a life of significance because God's got big plans, and they include you—I promise. And you know what else? It's not as complicated as you might think.

PART II

Aptitude to Astronauts

CHAPTER 9

Ass-Whoopin' or Ice Cream

If God is infallible and doesn't make mistakes,
why did he make me so messed up?

It may not seem like it, but most Americans still believe God exists and that He plays an active role in the lives of the people inhabiting this earth. In fact, almost eighty percent, according to most studies. If that's you, I'm guessing at some point, you've wondered if God created you for some specific purpose—a purpose greater than merely repopulating the earth. Have you ever thought this way?

I'd argue that the answer to every fundamental question in life, including this one, can be found in the Bible. And though it's not the only place you'll find this answer in the Bible, in the very last chapter of the very last book, God offers a conclusion of the 1,188 chapters that preceded it. In this final chapter, God reminds us, one last time, why He created us—He wants our praise. Whether or not you're a Christian, that probably sounds conceded, but stay with me.

The Bible says that God created us in His likeness or image. Of course, we are not deities—we're far from perfect, all-powerful, and all-knowing. We're not "like" God in that respect, but we are like God in many other ways. Some say being created in His likeness means we look like God physically, while others say our souls are like God's.

The older I get, the more I recognize how my relationship with God parallels my relationship with my mom and dad as their son. But also my relationship with my children as their father. People tell me I look like my dad, and sometimes they even mistakenly call me Dave. My sons are *like* me in many ways, yet at the same time, we're very different. But one thing's for sure: the relationship between my sons and me is amazingly similar to my relationship with God because He's my heavenly Father.

That brings us to another lofty question. Why do we, as human beings, desire to become parents? Well, I believe it's because we're created in God's likeness; it's instinctive. I'll take it one step further; I believe God gives us the innate desire to have children to understand better the relationship He wants to have with us.

But let's go back to my original question: Why did God create humans? God created us for the same reasons we instinctively want to have kids. It's to have a purpose and to be needed. It's to have a relationship and share experiences whereby we pass on worthwhile things we've learned. It's to be loved and honored, and, yes, we also instinctively desire to be parents because we long to be praised. The Bible says, *God inhabits our praises.* In other words, praising and honoring God is an excellent place to start if you want God to be a part of your life.

Praise is kind of an outdated word, at least by today's standards. But it's still easier to grasp than when the Bible refers to praising God as *fearing* Him. The "fear of the Lord" referenced in the Bible is closer to the relationship between a king and his subjects than what we think of when we hear the word fear today. Kings indeed ruled over people, but being the leader of a monarchy came with responsibility—the king protected his people from other countries.

So, in this context, fear is better defined as honor and respect. It's the same kind of fear most of us have for our earthly Fathers. Think back to your days on the playground when you might have said something like, "Oh yeah, well, my dad can beat up your dad." Now, you don't have a clue whether or not your dad can whoop your friend's dad, but you assume he can because he is your everything. And at the same time, in so many respects, he is your only thing. He's your protector, provider, teacher, and friend. As your parent, however, he is also your disciplinarian. So, there is a fear or reverence associated with our earthly Father.

To demonstrate my point, here's a true story from my childhood. I began taking piano lessons while I was in kindergarten. I can remember when it was time for my first recital. I sat on the front pew of Summerfield Methodist Church, a tiny church down the street from where we lived.

"The first student we will hear from today is also our youngest, Kevin McBroom," said my piano teacher as she gave me a smile of reassurance. I shook my head no, and other than that, I didn't move a muscle.

The teacher announced my name again, trying to maintain a sense of professionalism, "Ladies and gentlemen, I give you Kevin McBroom." I gave one hard head shake to the right and then back to the left.

My dad was seated somewhere several rows behind me. I'm guessing my teacher made eye contact with him and was grateful when he stood up and strolled down the aisle to give me some words of encouragement.

"Hey, Buddy." He always called me Buddy. "If you get up there and play your song, we'll go get the biggest ice cream cone you've ever had. And if you don't, I'm going to bust your ass."

Hmm, let me think. Ass-whoopin' or ice cream? Which do you think I picked?

I used to tell my sons that the world was not so different than when I was their age and that I understood what they were going through. But honestly, the more time passes, the less I feel like that's true anymore. Technology has changed the playing field. If we needed advice back in the '70s and '80s, we turned to friends and family we felt like we could trust. Today, however, we look at feedback ratings and reviews from total strangers. Young adults today, who have grown up on the

41

Internet, seek more direction in life from Google and YouTube than the Bible, their parents, and friends combined.

Social media is the ultimate social experiment for validation these days. We post things about our feelings, travels, jobs, or children, and we anxiously await approval from our "friends," many of whom we've never met in person. We repeatedly check for comments on our posts, and we hope it's so profound our friends will share it with their friends. If we get negative comments, we're devastated. We scroll through our list of *friends* to see if anyone has "unfriended" us. You probably know someone who says they "don't do" social media because they were offended by a friend's comment.

I like to call this insecurity complex the "Romper Room Effect." Back when I was a wee lad, Miss Nancy, the host of *The Romper Room* TV show, would hold up her Magic Mirror, which was nothing more than a mirror frame with no glass in it, and look out into "TV land" to see who was watching. "I can see Billy and Becky. I can see Susie and John. I can see Richard and Paula." She would name off half a dozen different kids. I would get on my knees about three feet from the TV screen and yell, "I'm right here! It's me, Kevin!" Then I would cry out, "She didn't see me."

I wish I could say all my insecurities stem from Miss Nancy's substandard Magic Mirror. But isn't it God's fault? I mean, after all, He made me this way. I used to ask myself, "If God is infallible and doesn't make mistakes, why did he make me so messed up?" Why am I starving for affirmation? And why do I desperately seek love, honor, and praise? Is any of this hitting close to home for you, too?

Well, if so, the good news is God has given us a guaranteed way to receive the validation we so desperately long for. The bad news is human behaviors like pride, greed, and lust tend to stand in the way. Case in point, remember in the last section how I misinterpreted The Parable of the Talents? A mixture of pride and greed clouded my understanding of what God was trying to show me.

But not to worry. Starting in the next chapter, I'll begin explaining how to correctly identify your *real* talents and why they're an essential part of what Jesus called an "abundant life."

CHAPTER 10

The Five-Talent Man

God has given us a divine assignment to "double our talents"—
the things that make us valuable.

When I decided to follow through and write this book, I attended a conference designed to help new writers like myself. Dexter Godfrey, one of the speakers at the meeting, entertained me thoroughly as he spoke about speaking—public speaking, to be exact. I don't remember everything he said, but I remember some of his points. For example, he used the acronym S.T.A.G.E. "S" stood for "stories stick." And he was right. As I sat through three days of "information overload," the memories I took home were predominately the stories from his presentation.

A parable is a story. It has riddle-like metaphors and often hidden meanings. A parable, by nature, is designed to make us think. All of us have sat through a lecture, presentation, or sermon, and the next day, we couldn't even remember the topic. And yet, you can remember the introductory joke or a story the speaker told. In fact, you remember it so well you share it with others. It may seem sad you didn't get more out of it, but that's how our brains work. So, it shouldn't be much of a surprise that the Creator of the universe understood the best way to teach His children was by telling stories.

In The Parable of the Talents, the master represents God, and the servants represent all of us. The master is going on a trip a long way away. We can assume he will be gone for a long time because, first, there were no jets or speedboats back then. And second, he made sure his stuff would be looked after while he was gone.

The master gave his "goods" to his three servants but didn't divvy them out equally. The parable says one servant got five talents, the second servant got two, and he gave one talent to the third servant. So why didn't each one get the same amount? Jesus said the master divided his goods based on *their ability*. Ability to do what? The ability of each servant to oversee these things called "talents."

A talent was an ancient unit of weight and measure in Greece, Rome, and the Middle East. As you progress through the New Testament, the term talent describes a coin or a specific amount of money. However, the use of the word talent in this parable is significant because, at that time, it was more than currency. Similar to using a bushel basket to measure grain or a gallon jug to measure milk, a talent was a container used to measure things of value or worth. It was most commonly used to measure precious metals but also other commodities like perfumes and spices. What's important to note is that anything that went inside the talent bowl was undoubtedly something of great value.

Now, back to our story as we fast forward to the master's return home. He called his three servants in and said something like, "So tell me what you did with the things I gave you to look after while I was away." The five-talent man said, "Well, I think you'll be happy with what I've done. I asked myself, if these goods were mine, what would I do with them? Then, an opportunity came along, and even though I had to put in a little extra effort, I was able to put the talents to good use, and believe it or not, I doubled them. So now, instead of the five talents, you have ten talents."

The master validated the actions of the five-talent servant by praising him. "Nice job. You've done so well with this assignment I'm going to put you in charge of something more important."

Next, the two-talent man came in and reported that he had done the same as the first, doubling the talents he was assigned to oversee. Again, the master validated the servant's efforts and told him he also should expect something more in the future.

But then we come to the accounting of the one-talent man. He admitted to the master that he had buried the single talent because he was afraid. Understandably, I guess. At least he was honest, right? But the master was upset. He didn't care that the servant had been anxious about his assignment. He even called the servant wicked and lazy. The master took the single talent from the servant and gave it to the servant, who had doubled his five talents, meaning he now had eleven to oversee.

I'm embarrassed to share this with you. Nevertheless, when I first studied this story, I honestly believed God was instructing me to double my financial investments. And if I were afraid to do so, He would label me wicked and lazy, too. At that time in my life, pretty much all of my goals were focused on business and investments. So, for me, the parable was like a confirmation from God himself that I was on the right track.

Isn't it interesting that from all of the options He had, Jesus chose to tell this story using the talent? I like to think He did so intentionally because of the double meaning of the word talent. But maybe that's just because I know it will make me feel better about completely missing what Jesus was trying to convey in the parable.

It wasn't until the poop hit the proverbial fan, and we had lost so much financially, that I began to question my understanding of the parable. Ultimately, I discovered the figurative was, in fact, literal. I mean, do you honestly believe God would chastise us for not doubling our money? Of course not. It was idiotic for me ever to consider that in the first place. But God does expect us to double what makes us valuable: our God-given talents—the *goods* God gives us that equip us for our purpose in life.

I grew up hearing little boys are made of "snips and snails and puppy dog tails," while it's "sugar and spice and everything nice" running through the veins of little girls. But no two boys and no two girls are the same, are they? Not even close. We were designed uniquely by God on purpose.

It's not always easy to identify what makes us so unique. Fortunately, there are lots of tools out there to help us figure it out. Because it's pretty hard to grow something if you're not even sure how to identify it, so that's what we will focus on in the following few chapters. Then, in chapter 15, I'll introduce you to a new way to approach life. It's derived from one of my favorite movies, *Apollo 13*.

I have to forewarn you these upcoming four chapters are a bit meatier than the previous ones. So, if you start to feel overwhelmed with the material, you have my permission to skip to chapter 15, *Apollo 13 Engineering*.

CHAPTER 11

——

That Boy's Got Talent

You are the only person created to do what God has planned for you to do in your lifetime.

As a kid growing up in the 1970s, television was my life. Fortunately, there were only four channels to choose from back then, and they "signed off" at midnight. On Saturday mornings, you knew right where to find me—sitting on our luxurious, shag-carpeted living room floor with my nose six feet from the TV.

After the School House Rock and Looney Tunes reruns had ended, I'd ride my bicycle around our neighborhood until the banana seat chafed my buttocks. Yet, I always seemed to be sitting back in front of the TV, legs crossed, just about the time ABC's *Wide World of Sports* came on channel 2.

"Spanning the globe to bring you the constant variety of sport; the thrill of victory; and the agony of defeat; the human drama of athletic competition." The familiar voice of Jim McKay, along with the iconic crash of ski jumper Vinko Bogataj, let you know you were about to witness an hour-and-a-half of unscripted entertainment. Men and women, some from countries I'd never heard of, were about to display talents I'd never dreamed possible.

The show covered traditional Olympic events, like gymnastics, boxing, and track and field. But I didn't come back inside before dark on a Saturday afternoon to watch figure skating. No, I wanted to see the more exotic competitions that were sometimes hard to label as sports at all. Things like lumberjack log-rolling, Acapulco cliff diving, and, of course, barrel jumping on ice skates.

Why did they do it? Why did they risk getting severely injured or worse? Was it to test their skills or for fame and fortune? Was it the stereotypical "guy trying to impress the girls?" Of course, we've all tried things to test our abilities. I'm sure someone rode a cow entirely out of curiosity long before it drew a crowd of cheering fans. By the way, for that person, it really was their "first rodeo." Ha! I couldn't resist.

We often think of talents as falling into one or more of these three categories: physical, mental, or creative. Webster's Dictionary defines talent as *a special, often athletic, creative, or artistic aptitude; a general intelligence or mental power or ability*.

When I was in school, students flaunted their physical talents while hiding their mental abilities. Why? Because the athletes were praised and honored. Maybe your school was different, but at my school, getting labeled a "brainiac" was a surefire way to get made fun of, especially if you were a boy. The jocks received the lion's share of the attention. All the kids wanted to be like them. Heck, I wanted to be like them. I questioned why God made me undersized and uncoordinated.

My wife, Pam, was the oldest of three children and took on a mothering-type role for her younger sister and brother, as many older siblings do. Her sister and brother excelled at sports, and Pam was their biggest supporter. The more accolades they received, the less she focused on *her* achievements, proudly living out her dreams through their accomplishments. Honestly, as her boyfriend, I grew tired of hearing Pam brag about her sister and brother's successes. She was like a proud momma and never showed any signs of feeling like she had missed out.

In Chapter 3, I described how, in the late 1980s, I had written down a list of things I would like to accomplish if I had no shortage of ability or support. Pam made a similar list. Unfortunately, I only remember a few of the items on her list. But there are a couple I'll *never* forget.

"Meet Sean Connery." I couldn't help but chuckle when I first read this on Pam's list. I was already mentally prepared for the day my wife might leave me for James Bond. She had told me many times that if he ever *came-a-knocking*, she'd kick me to the curb in a heartbeat. But then, I read a goal on my young bride's list that ended my laughter and put a lump in my throat, "Be good at anything." Now, obviously, there's nothing funny about that. I had known this sweet little girl intimately for over five years. But, apparently, I still had a few things to learn about the love of my life.

Pam was not a good sister; she was a great sister. She was also a great daughter, wife, and school teacher. Compared to me and all of the people I knew, she was as near to flawless as any person out there—she still is. Pam was talented at things that *really* matter in life, just not those that tend to bring praise and honor. And though no one else seemed to notice, it obviously bothered her. She had successfully kept her wounded spirit hidden from her friends, family, and even from me, her husband.

I share this story because it's valid for so many. I've heard it referred to as "The Comparison Trap," or how we measure up to the accomplishments of others. The problem with this mindset is that it's a *no-win* situation. When we compare ourselves to others, we tend to fall into one of two traps.

The first trap happens when we measure our perceived accomplishments, abilities, or successes to those we view as better than ourselves. This type of assessment often causes us to have thoughts like, *I'll never be as successful as they are, so what's the use of trying?*

The second trap comes when we measure our perceived accomplishments, abilities, or successes against others who can't seem to get anything right in life. This comparison can stifle our personal development by killing our motivation to be all God created us to be. We might find ourselves thinking something like, *Compared to them, I'm a superstar. I guess I should kick back and take it easy.*

God did not create you to compare yourself to others. Even *He* doesn't compare you to others. Why? Because you are the only person created to do what God has planned for you to do in your lifetime. That's why we must identify and understand our God-given talents. Let me demonstrate my point.

Although it's impossible to measure with any certainty, it's safe to assume that at this very moment, there are two collegiate wrestlers who started their high school wrestling careers with almost identical measures of physical, mental, and creative skills as it pertains to grappling. Suppose all other influencers are equal, things like family support, coaching, etc. Why will one athlete outperform and achieve more than the other, often by leaps and bounds?

I recently had the pleasure of meeting Olympic Gold Medal Wrestler Kyle Snyder. I watched as over a hundred people stood in line to have their picture taken with this humble young man. They showered him with praises. I didn't ask Kyle, but I'd bet he knows someone who was every bit his equal during their freshman year in high school. A teenager with the same measure of physical, mental, and creative skills Kyle had back then, and on paper, was his equal.

But with time, Kyle's success overshadowed the other wrestler. You see, there's more to it than our outward talents. We all possess other talents, even if we don't realize it. Sadly, many people don't, and they find themselves stuck in the comparison trap, throwing up their hands and thinking, *What's the use?* But we can exchange disappointment for enthusiasm simply by understanding how God has given us talents enabling us to achieve feats more extraordinary than those that earn Olympic Gold.

The God-given talents I am referring to are spiritual. Kyle is obviously physically, mentally, and creatively talented as a wrestler. But he is also spiritually gifted to fulfill his true purpose. Now, he may *think* that his purpose in life is to be the best wrestler in the world. But chances are, that's only part of God's plan for his life—and it's certainly not his purpose.

In the remainder of this book, we will discuss the things that separate Olympic medal winners from those who allow fears and failures to hold them back. I've intentionally tried not to make this book too *churchy* by over-spiritualizing things. But, there is no way to water down the supernatural aspects of what the Bible identifies as our spiritual gifts.

These gifts are nothing like the natural talents you think of when describing Albert Einstein, Michelangelo, or Kyle Snyder. They rarely bring the praise and honor that comes with winning a gold medal. Instead, the talents I'm talking about are divine in nature, and they enable us to carry out *God's plan* and fulfill *our purpose* in life regardless of our physical, mental, and creative abilities.

CHAPTER 12

God-Given Gifts

You may fantasize about being a superhero.
But God wants us to be supernatural heroes.

As I implied in the previous chapter, it often takes more than physical, mental, and creative talents to stand out and succeed in life. At least in the areas that really matter, or *should* matter. Because we're all born with unique strengths that we underutilize and weaknesses we struggle to overcome. But beneath it all lies something the Bible calls spiritual gifts. These gifts are our foundational talents and where our primary focus must be to truly live a life of significance.

Spiritual gifts are identified in three different places in the Bible: 1 Corinthians 12, Ephesians 4, and Romans 12. These lists have varying applications, and while the gifts are unique for the most part, a few overlap. But if you don't count the duplications, there are 19 spiritual gifts in all.

The seven gifts listed in Romans 12:6-8 are called the *motivational gifts*. They are the jumping-off point for the other gifts listed in Corinthians and Ephesians and, again, what I refer to as our foundational talents. Here are the verses from Romans 12, where the gifts are listed:

6   *Having then gifts differing according to the grace that is given to us, let us use them: if prophecy, let us prophesy in proportion to our faith;*

7   *Or ministry, let us use it in our ministering; he who teaches, in teaching;*

8   *He who exhorts, in exhortation; he who gives, with liberality; he who leads, with diligence; he who shows mercy, with cheerfulness.*

Of course, this was written around 2000 years ago, and sometimes, the more traditional translations of the Bible are pretty challenging to follow. So, to clarify, the spiritual gifts are *prophecy, ministry, teaching, exhortation, giving, leading, and showing mercy.*

Several good books in print today cover the topic of spiritual gifts. Many have tests or guides to help you identify and apply your specific gift(s). But, hands down, my favorite book on this subject is the simply-titled perennial *Discover Your God-Given Gifts* by Don and Katie Fortune.

The Fortunes chose to use more common words for some of the gifts listed in Romans 12. Below is their list, along with portions of the definition they give for each:

1. Perceiver - (in place of prophecy or prophet) one who clearly perceives the will of God.

2. Server - (in place of ministry or minister) one who loves to serve others. Another appropriate word is "doer."

3. Teacher - one who loves to research and communicate truth. We almost selected the word "researcher."

4. Exhorter - one who loves to encourage others to live a victorious life. These are extremely positive people who can equally well be called "encouragers."

5. Giver - one who loves to give time, talent, energy, and means to benefit others and advance the Gospel. Another word could be "contributor."

6. Administrator - one who loves to organize, lead, or direct. Other words could be "facilitator" and "leader."

7. Compassion person - (in place of mercy) one who shows compassion, love, and care to those in need.

In their book, the Fortune's list 20 characteristics for each of the seven gifts, followed by an in-depth discussion of those characteristics. The book walks you through a self-administered assessment to build a personal profile of your giftings. Negative traits that sometimes arise in people possessing a particular gift are also assessed. Based on your personal profile scores, the book offers insight, advice, and suggestions for where you will most likely find success in ministry and vocation.

If you've never used a personal development resource to better understand God's plan for your life, I encourage you to try it. I believe *Discover Your God-Given Gifts* is a great place to invest your time and money. I don't make anything from endorsing their book—but I'm a huge fan. You can find the book wherever books are sold or visit www.discoveryourgifts.org for more information.

You'll be surprised at what you learn as you look beneath the surface of your assumptions about yourself. For instance, my wife Pam has been a teacher for about a hundred years (that's a joke, of course). So, you would think that her top spiritual gift would be Teaching. But you'd be wrong.

In fact, when she took the assessments found in *Discover Your God-Given Gifts*, the gift of teaching scored lowest. From this, you might assume she's unhappy with her career choice. But again, you'd be wrong. Pam loves her job. So much so that I highly doubt she would ever consider doing anything else.

Remember, someone whose gift is teaching is typically a gifted researcher, which my Pam is not. Her primary spiritual gift is compassion, closely followed by a tie in the gifts of serving and exhortation. Pam teaches middle school, and I think it'd be hard to find a group of individuals in greater need of compassion and encouragement than a bunch of preteens in full bloom.

Now, because it's all she's ever done, Pam might assume teaching is the only vocation she would enjoy. However, since God gifted her to serve, encourage, and show compassion, she would also likely excel working as a nurse, therapist, receptionist, customer service representative, or even a missionary. Hopefully, you're beginning to see the importance yet unpredictability of identifying your spiritual talents.

Suppose I asked you what would make someone a good teacher. You might say, "Someone who has in-depth knowledge of a subject and the skills to assist students in understanding and retaining that information." But what if I asked you what makes a teacher *great*? You might add to your earlier answer, "Someone who motivates and encourages" or "Someone who recognizes and serves each student's individual needs."

Today, comic book characters are some of the most popular personalities in movies. You may fantasize about being a superhero. But God wants us to be *supernatural* heroes. So let me encourage you again to identify your talents and embrace them for what they are—your *superpowers*.

There's a lot of debate over spiritual gifts, and I respect that because they're less important than the core beliefs of Christianity (salvation, resurrection, etc.). But if you're a believer and already embrace the notion of what is commonly called the gifts of the Holy Spirit, I'd like to suggest an additional resource for discovering your spiritual gifts. It's an online test called *spiritualgiftstest.com,* and it's free, which is always nice.

Pastor Jeff Carver is the mastermind behind this website, which has been operating for over a decade. Carver combines all 19 of the spiritual gifts in this assessment. It's quick and easy, and there are follow-up materials for sale on the site to take you on a deeper dive, should you choose to do so. I'd label this site a "201" course, while *Discover Your God-Given Gifts* is more of a "101" course. Keep that in mind when deciding which resource best suits your needs.

The book you are currently reading is less about identifying your talents and more about applying them. However, in the *Applications* section at the back of this book, I've included an abbreviated version of the *Discover Your God-Given Gifts* assessment. Hopefully, this will help to identify your own God-given gifts and create a hunger for a more in-depth understanding of their role in your life.

Remember, one of our basic needs is to receive praise and honor. The best way to ensure you're getting what you need in this area is to receive validation from God by doubling your spiritual talents. That's why Pam truly enjoys a thankless job like teaching, even though it seldom brings her a pat on the back. She doesn't need validation from others when she uses her God-given gifts. More often than not, relying on others to stroke our egos leads to disappointment.

In the following two chapters, we will take a closer look at what lies just above the surface of our foundational talents—our personality. Maybe you've taken a personality assessment before. It's become commonplace in business because it helps determine how new team members will *work and play* with others. So if you're a personality assessment junkie like I am, feel free to skip over to Chapter 15. But suppose your spouse or close friends occasionally suggest you need to work on your social skills. If that's the case, it might be a good idea to turn the page and dive into the following two chapters.

CHAPTER 13

———

I'm Mean

If you don't have special needs, you shouldn't be especially needy.

t was a sunny Sunday afternoon. I was making one of my bimonthly drives up I-75 to our business in Tennessee. On this particular trip, I was listening to the book *Will It Fly?* by Pat Flynn. Before Pat became an author and host of the podcast *Smart Passive Income,* he wanted to be an architect. A large firm in San Francisco hired him immediately out of college as a drafter. In his book, he shares an important lesson learned during his tenure at the firm.

His supervisor was a director in the organization, so his time was always in high demand. But this didn't keep him from lording over his new hires. Sometimes, he would question Pat's performance and embarrass him in front of his peers. Pat assumed his boss didn't like him until, one day, he called him into his office. "Patrick, do you know why I call you out?"

Pat wanted to answer, "Because you're a cyborg from the future?" But, instead, he replied, "No, why?"

"Because I want you to succeed as an architect." He explained, showing Pat he genuinely cared about his future.

Then, he gave Pat a directive that, at the time, seemed overbearing. "Whenever I ask you a question, Patrick, I want you to respond in one sentence—that's all you get. Think about what you need to say in one sentence to convey all the necessary items to help me understand exactly what's going on. One sentence—nothing more."

Listening to Pat's story reminded me of an all-too-familiar situation going on in our little company in Tennessee. We had a young lady working with us, and like Pat at the architectural firm, she was very new on the job. She was also about twenty years younger than the rest of her coworkers, which probably made things awkward for her in and of itself.

Almost every time I spoke with this employee, it felt like she was trying to prove herself to me. Simple questions often resulted in long conversations where she would insist on explaining why she had chosen to do things the way she had. So I started calling my other employees on their cell phones, hoping to avoid the possibility of her answering the phone and cornering me into another time-wasting discussion.

At this point in Pat's story, I paused the audiobook and called my business partner. "Hey man, I'm listening to this book, and it's got me thinking." I then explained the one-sentence directive described in Flynn's book and how I thought a similar approach might work for our newest hire.

"How do you think she will receive a message like this?" I asked. "After all, you'll have to live with the aftermath if it doesn't go well."

"I like it," he said. "There's a chance she'll get her feelings hurt, but I think it's worth the risk. She's always trying to justify her actions, which kind of wears everybody out. I constantly have to cut her off mid-sentence, and I can tell it irritates her. But I'm just too busy to listen beyond the point of what I need to know. I don't want to fire her because everybody here likes her, and I can only assume things will get better with time—if she doesn't quit first.

As I drove, I mentally charted my talking points—mapping out the words I hoped would persuade this young lady to develop new habits. Then, the following day, I asked her to come to my office to talk.

"Do you know the biggest difference between you and me?" I asked.

The question was rhetorical, so I wasn't expecting her to answer. But before I could start framing the words I had just spoken, she replied, "You're mean?" Her inflection told me she was waiting for me to indicate if she had answered correctly.

"Um, no, dear," I said, reeling from the verbal uppercut. "The biggest difference between you and me is, *you* are a woman, and *I* am a man. God made us different, and it's a scientific fact that women use more words than men to communicate." I was trying to set a tone of acceptance and understanding, but I wasn't succeeding.

Nevertheless, I continued to shove my foot deeper into my mouth, "So while you *think* everyone here is mad at you when they ask you to hurry up and get to the point, that's not the case. You see, it's because *we* (I gestured by spreading my arms wide and moving my hands about with palms up as if I was speaking for everyone) are all a bunch of grumpy old men who want *you* to get to the point so *we* can get back to work and take care of our customers. It's not that we don't like or care about you, but the way you communicate keeps us from meeting our deadlines."

You know how sometimes you see things playing out differently in your mind? This was one of those occasions. No matter how hard I tried, I just seemed to make things worse. She went from confused, to angry, to crying, all within about ten minutes. I handed her a box of Kleenex and thought to myself *I should've just bought her the stinking book.*

As I pointed out in the previous chapter, our spiritual gifts are the foundational talents on which our personality traits are built. That may not seem significant until you recognize that all seven God-given spiritual gifts are designed to help others. In contrast, our personalities determine how we approach situations and interact with others. In other words, our spiritual gifts focus on the needs of others, while our personality traits concentrate more on our own needs.

I like to think of it like this: Our spiritual gifts are similar to the foundation of a building—they lie beneath the surface. So, it's hard to make out their shape and form. And maybe that's a good thing because changing them would be extremely difficult, if not impossible.

On the other hand, our personalities are like a building sitting on top of that foundation, exposed for all to see. Think of your personality as a house built the year you were born. Some elements of your older home are considered desirable because they're classic, weathered, or rustic. But just because you're happy with the way your house looks, functions, and flows doesn't mean others share in your opinions. And that's okay if they're simply judging the outside of your home as they drive past.

But what if someone you know needed a place to stay for a while, and you seized the opportunity to make some extra money and rented them a room? Suddenly, this person's opinion, who you'll now be interacting with daily, matters a great deal. Because maybe what you call rustic, they call rough, and issues that don't bother you anymore are unacceptable to them. Sure, it's your house, and it's functional, for the most part, but chances are your new renter will expect you to compromise and make some changes. Oh, and they'll probably remind you about these needed changes every day until you start making some improvements.

Of course, we're not actually talking about houses or roommates, are we? The truth is not everyone will like who you are, what you think, or how you react to things. And again, that's not a big deal until that someone suddenly becomes an active part of your life, like your child's teacher, your mother-in-law, or a hyper-sensitive employee who talks too much. Too often, we neglect our weaknesses, and things begin to deteriorate gradually without us recognizing them. Unfortunately, we often don't notice until someone is bold enough to point it out.

But not to worry, because our personalities are not foundational like our spiritual gifts; they're more what I would call structural. So, even though it will require some serious alterations, our personalities can be improved upon, updated, and even remodeled.

Look, I don't *think* I'm mean. But my opinion about myself is only half of the equation. When it comes to personality or character traits, we all have strengths and weaknesses. And even though we may want to believe it's just who we are, and people need to get over it, what other people think about us matters. For instance, in the situation with my employee, her opinion is what matters most. Why? Because I was asking her to make a change, not the other way around.

Now, do you want to know what's embarrassing? I've spent countless hours studying all of this personality stuff, so I understand the importance of identifying what makes others "tick" and how to "speak their language." For example, I figured out a long time ago that I tend to rub people the wrong way, yet still, on that day, I handled the situation like an insensitive amateur.

My inability to effectively communicate with this young lady proves how important it is to view our personalities like the house in which we live. If we want others to like it as much as we do, we need to know it inside and out. Then, hopefully, we can recognize when things require some maintenance or remodeling, especially whenever you choose to open the door and invite someone else to come into your life.

CHAPTER 14

Just the Way I'm Wired

Thank heavens there is only one of everyone.

While working at my dad's body shop, he decided we needed to do some team building among middle management. So, he hired a business coach and called everyone in for a weekend conference. The first thing this coach had us do was a personality assessment.

Now, I don't think my dad was intentionally cheating. But, it was obvious that he was choosing answers he thought would make him look better to his employees. I called "bull crap" the first couple of times he shared his answers with the group, but I stopped when I realized I was embarrassing him. After all, it was the first time my father had ever participated in an assessment like this. It's a common mistake to skew your answers, especially when you know you'll be sharing them with others.

Our innate desire to be validated can obstruct us from identifying our weaknesses. That's precisely why personality assessments are so valuable. We all think we know "who we are" inside and out. But in reality, we do an outstanding job of convincing ourselves we're either better or worse than we actually are. Trust me; it's more complicated than sugar and spice, and everything nice. I've yet to meet anyone who didn't learn something about themselves by participating in this type of exercise.

The corporate world realized a long time ago the importance of identifying personalities when it comes to hiring, sales training, and improving team culture. Today, there's an entire industry devoted to helping businesses identify individuals' strengths and weaknesses. As an employer and business coach, I've used many of these assessments personally and professionally. There are a lot of options out there—perhaps too many. Some are free, but as the old saying goes, "You get what you pay for."

Popular tests like *Strengthsfinder 2.0, Meyers-Briggs Type Indicator*, and the *Enneagram* all require some sort of financial investment. They run anywhere from $12 to $60, depending on where and how you access them. For those who want more, most offer additional resources that dig deeper into your character and, of course, your wallet.

For many years, I preferred an assessment called the *DISC Profile*. You can buy *DISC* through many third-party sources such as a business or life coach. This resource groups personality into four primary distinctions: Dominance, Influence, Steadiness, and Conscientiousness—thus the acronym D-I-S-C.

DISC also determines a secondary designation. The first letter from each designator is used to reference your personality type. For instance, my designation is

D.I., with "D" representing Dominance as my primary trait and "I" or Influence as my secondary. I'm partial to the labeling system of *DISC* because, with only four primary categories, it's easy to learn and remember them. In addition, having fewer designations to memorize can be helpful when quickly identifying the personalities of others.

But my favorite assessment comes from the book titled *Wired That Way* by Marita Littauer. This resource is less current than some of today's more popular options. Nevertheless, I often recommend this assessment over others for three reasons. First, the system follows a similar pattern to The DISC, using only four primary categories. Second, Littauer focuses on how positive and negative character traits affect your personal life and relationships at home and work. Finally, Littauer does an excellent job of putting all the information into a Christian-based context. I find this helpful when meshing my personality traits with my spiritual gifts.

I realize this may be getting a bit dry for some of you, so before we move on, I want to take a moment and ask you to do something. I'm about to introduce you to the concepts found in Littauer's book. Rather than merely reading the material, I'd like you to identify the character traits that define how *you* are wired. Trust me; it will be fun. Now, let's begin.

Listed below are the personality types used in the *Wired That Way* assessment. Notice each of the four types is made up of two descriptive words. Beneath those is a list of the dominant traits associated with each type. For example, "Basic Desire" lists the overarching goal of someone with that personality type. Next are the "Emotional Needs," which point out what a person with that personality type is looking for in a relationship. Finally, "Controls By" tells us how someone with this personality type might react when they feel like they're losing control of a situation.

Remember, as you read the "makeup" of each type, think about which best describes your personality.

Powerful Choleric

- Basic Desire: *Have control.*
- Emotional Needs: *Loyalty, sense of control, appreciation, credit for work.*
- Controls By: *Threat of anger.*

Popular Sanguine

- Basic Desire: *Have fun.*
- Emotional Needs: *Attention, affection, approval, acceptance.*
- Controls By: *Charm.*

Perfect Melancholy

- Basic Desire: *Have perfection.*
- Emotional Needs: *Sensitivity, support, space, silence.*
- Controls By: *Threat of moods.*

Peaceful Phlegmatic

- Basic Desire: *Have peace.*
- Emotional Needs: *Peace and quiet, feeling of worth, lack of stress, respect.*
- Controls By: *Procrastination.*

So, how'd it go? As you went through those traits, did you find yourself thinking *yep, that's me?*

The first word of each of the *Wired That Way* personality types is a commonly used adjective. For instance, everyone knows what I mean when I say someone is trying to be powerful, popular, perfect, or peaceful. But Littauer's choices for the second descriptors aren't words used in everyday conversation. So let's define them, and as you read these definitions, see if anyone you know comes to mind.

- Choleric: *Bad-tempered or irritable.*
- Sanguine: *Optimistic or positive, especially in a bad or difficult situation.*
- Melancholy: *Sad and pensive (pensive means involving deep or serious thought).*
- Phlegmatic: *Having an unemotional and calm disposition.*

I'll bet it didn't take long before friends or family members started popping into your head as you read those definitions. So now, let me pose a different question. Which of the above four would your friends or family say best describes *you?*

You may be wondering why I'm spending so much time talking about spiritual gifts and personality traits. I get it; it can be a lot to digest. Plus, it probably seems insignificant compared to fulfilling your purpose in life. So let me explain. It's hard to put into words, but there's something almost magical about seeing in black-and-white words describing who you are with such accuracy and precision. It's as if a detective has been following you around for years, documenting your every thought.

I want you to experience this discovery for yourself, to see firsthand how genuinely enlightening it can be. This knowledge brings an unexplainable sense of peace about who God made you to be. It's like you've been given permission to take ownership of your strengths and weaknesses. But more importantly, it gives you the wisdom to know what you should and should not take on in life.

So, if you've not taken the time to understand your personality traits and spiritual gifts fully, please make it happen. You won't be sorry. I promise it will make you a better person and strengthen your relationships, not only with your friends and family but with God as well.

We're almost ready to move on to the next section, where I'll be sharing the meaning of life with you. And no, I'm not kidding—I'm serious.

But first, I want to share something with you that I believe you'll find truly inspiring. I call it *Apollo 13 Engineering* and it has become my barometer in life and business. Because in addition to our natural talents, spiritual gifts, and personality strengths and weaknesses, we all have tangible, more definable assets at our disposal. So, turn the page and get ready to see things in a whole new way.

CHAPTER 15

———

Apollo 13 Engineering

God has given us everything we need to succeed.
It's already at our disposal.

The 1995 Ron Howard movie *Apollo 13* tells the real-life story of a near-catastrophic space mission undertaken by astronauts Jim Lovell, Fred Haise, and Jack Swigert. Two of the three men were supposed to walk on the moon during that mission. Instead, all three wound up fighting just to make it home alive.

Before Apollo 13 reached the moon, an explosion left the ship disabled and running dangerously low on power and oxygen. So NASA devised a plan to use the Lunar Module as a shuttle to return the astronauts home safely. But the Lunar Module was designed to carry two men to the moon's surface, not three men back to Earth. Moreover, the additional carbon dioxide expelled by the third astronaut's breathing was more than the Lunar Module could filter. NASA had to come up with a solution, and fast, or the men would die from CO2 poisoning.

The larger filters from the disabled Command Module were adequate to filter out the dangerous gas. However, because different companies manufactured the two modules, the filters weren't interchangeable. The filters for the Lunar Module were about the size of a loaf of bread and cylinder-shaped, while the filters for the Command Module were square and shaped like a school lunch box.

In my favorite scene from the movie, every available piece of nonessential equipment on the Lunar Module was dumped out on a conference table at NASA's Mission Control. A handful of engineers stood encircling the table filled with the items. One of the men held up a round filter in one hand and a square filter in the other, then gave them their marching orders.

"Okay, people, listen up," he begins. "The people upstairs handed us this one, and we've got to come through. We've got to find a way to make this (the square filter) fit into the hole for this (the round filter) using nothing but that." He motions to all the items on the table. "Okay, let's get it organized," he says as they start sorting through all the stuff.

In a vacuum, this is a snapshot of our everyday lives. In its simplest form, I've never come across a better parallel. You can compartmentalize it into categories like marriage, work, or relationships if it helps you wrap your head around it. Let's use child-rearing as an example.

We have to raise our kids using what we have today. What other people are doing—their successes, failures, and advice—may give you insight. But *your* kids are different, and the available time you have is different, and your finances are different, and your level of intelligence is different, and your strengths and weaknesses are different.

Look at it this way: your table of stuff, or the things you have to work with, looks very different from everyone else's table, and chances are tomorrow it won't be the same as today. You may have more stuff, or you may have less. It may be better stuff, or it may be worse. But today, whatever is on your table is all you've got to work with.

The same is true for your workplace, marriage, and everything else in life. Sometimes, there are days when I'm discouraged and quick to be negative, and I tell myself, "I'll never reach my goals unless God gives me more to work with."

Can He give me more? Sure, He can. But will He? It goes back to the parallel we looked at in Chapter 9, where I shared my belief that God instinctively provides us with a desire to have children so we might better understand His relationship with us as His children.

When raising my sons, there were times I could have helped them more. It was within my means. They never realized I was debating whether or not I should step in and help. All of us have been there, whether with a child, family member, friend, or co-worker.

Have you ever watched a baby getting frustrated because she couldn't do something, and when the mom started to rush in and help, someone stopped her and said, "Wait, see if she can figure it out on her own?"

Even though the child gives up, stretches out her little arms, gives mom a puppy-dog look, and whines, "Mommy, help." What happens?

Mom does help, just not physically. "You can do it," she says in that loving way that only a mom can say without being patronizing. It's not about what the child wants—immediate physical assistance. It's about what the child needs for long-term advancement—verbal encouragement.

This opportunity opens the door for every parent's starring role, cheerleader, or exhorter, as we learned in chapter 12. "Yay! You did it!" Mom cheers, clapping her hands. What's the response from the baby girl? She repeatedly accomplishes the task, soaking up her mom's affirmation.

Again, I'm no theologian, but I'd bet my last banana that God is "raising" us in the same manner. So, we need to go out into the world daily, reminding ourselves that God's grace is sufficient to meet all our needs. Therefore, we know He has given us everything we need to succeed. It's already at our disposal, waiting for us on our "table of stuff."

Still, it's our job to figure out how to make that square peg fit into the round hole. Today, I have faith that God has given me everything I need, and He is anxiously waiting for the opportunity to tell me, "Well done." That's my hope and prayer for you, too—to understand and believe that God has equipped you to fulfill your purpose in life.

And speaking of your purpose, I promised I'd share that with you in the next section, didn't I? Well, congratulations. You've finally made it. So, what are we waiting for?

PART III

Purpose to Passion

CHAPTER 16

The One Thing—Well,
Two Things—No, Actually Three

God may have different plans for each of us,
but...we all have the same purpose...

One of my all-time favorite movies is *City Slickers*. In the movie, Billy Crystal plays a guy going through a mid-life crisis. Crystal and his two best friends head out west to a dude ranch, driving cattle, riding horses, and sleeping under the stars. A seasoned cowboy, played by the late, great Jack Palance, leads the cattle drive, and in one scene, Crystal and Palance are slowly riding along, talking about life. But then Palance stops his horse and says to Crystal, "You know what the secret of life is?"

"No, what?"

Palance holds up his index finger. "This," he says.

Crystal looks confused. "Your finger?"

"One thing. Just one thing," Palance clarifies. "You stick to that, and everything else don't mean crap."

"That's great. But what's the one thing?"

As he rides away, Palance says, "That's what you've got to figure out."

All of us, sooner or later, figure out that we need to figure *it* out, and the sooner we figure *that* out, the better off we'll be—you can quote me on that. But seriously, maybe that's why you're reading this book. Regardless of our spiritual beliefs, at some point, we all find ourselves questioning the significance of our existence, and even though you can't quite put your finger on it, you know that something is missing in your life.

There's lots of "noise" out there today trying to convince us that we don't measure up. Nevertheless, if we make enough money, hang out with the right people, drink a particular brand of beer, drive a nicer car, and change how we dress, we'll not only be accepted by those we're trying to impress, but all of our insecurities will disappear. Unfortunately, worldly validation is a moving target, and it's impossible to hit with any consistency.

And that's why Jack Palance was right. The secret to life is one thing—one word, actually. That doesn't mean this secret is straightforward or easy to master. No, quite the opposite. And maybe that's why it's discussed so thoroughly throughout the New Testament of the Bible.

I have no way of proving this, but I think God makes the truly important things complex on purpose. Let me explain. Many times, I've read passages in the Bible, and I found them so clear and understandable that I could apply them to my life immediately. And yet, years later, I will reread those same scriptures, and they take on a different or broader meaning. It's as if the words in the Bible are alive and transform to fit every season of our lives.

But not all of the Bible is so fluid. Did you know there are 613 laws written in the Old Testament? Some Jewish people still do their best to follow all of them. Kind of hard to imagine, huh? Maybe that explains why there's a story in the Bible about a religious man who asked Jesus this question:

36 *"Teacher, which is the great commandment in the law?"*

37 *Jesus said to him," 'You shall love the Lord your God with all your heart, with all your soul, and with all your mind.'*

38 *This is the first and great commandment.*

39 *And the second is like it: 'You shall love your neighbor as yourself.'*

40 *On these two commandments hang all the Law and the Prophets."*

Matthew 22:36-40 New King James Version (NKJV)

I'm guessing the man who asked Jesus which commandment was most important was expecting one of the Ten Commandments to be Jesus' answer. But Jesus tended to answer questions in unexpected ways. In fact, when asked, he didn't choose *any* of the commandments or laws. Instead, He summed up all the laws with these two open-ended directives—love God and love others.

It's important to note that Jesus could have chosen to tell the man the single greatest commandment is to love God, period, end of statement. But Jesus didn't stop there. He threw in that other part about loving your neighbor as yourself. It's as if Jesus, the son of God, explained that we can't fulfill one without doing the other. I have to admit I found this a bit perplexing at first.

To better understand the reasoning behind Jesus' answer, we need to go back and put The Parable of the Talents into the proper context by looking at the Words that come before and after the parable. The 25th chapter of Matthew is made up of three stories told by Jesus. I will take a little liberty and paraphrase them to save time. But if you'd like to read them for yourself, you can find Matthew 25 before Chapter 1 at the front of this book.

The first story (Matthew 25:1-13) is The Parable of the Ten Virgins, highlighting the ancient tradition of Jewish weddings. In this story, ten virgin bridesmaids await the bridegroom's arrival to mark the beginning of the marriage festival. However, they don't know when he will arrive—it could be days, months, or even years.

Five of the virgins remain passionately prepared for the bridegroom's return. But the other five virgins are so caught up in their day-to-day lives that they're completely caught off guard when they learn the bridegroom is about to arrive. They ask the prepared group of virgins for help, but there isn't time. So, only half of the bridesmaids get to attend the festival.

At the most basic level, I think Jesus is telling us "It's okay to live for today, but don't lose sight of the big picture. Because if you're not careful, you'll wake up one day and realize your life would have been so much better if you'd focused more on having a relationship with Me. But it has to be a genuine relationship. A lot of people *say* they follow Me. But, only half of my followers will get to experience the full, abundant life I've custom-tailored for them."

Our response to this warning should be something like, "Holy Cow! That's not good. What should I do?"

Then Jesus shares the second parable (Matthew 25:14-30), The Parable of the Talents. In this story, Jesus essentially says God made everyone unique on purpose because our lives have a unique purpose. Therefore, we need to be passionate about doubling what makes us valuable—our talents. Then, when we faithfully use what God has given us to work with, He'll open doors to new opportunities and experiences.

Our response to this story should be, "Wow, that sounds awesome. But how do I know I'm doing what I'm supposed to be—living *faithfully?*"

Jesus answers that question for us in the final part of Matthew 25, verses 31-46, which, interestingly, is His last documented teaching before being arrested and crucified. This final story illustrates the end of times when Jesus brings all His followers together and divides them into two groups. Jesus then turns to one of the groups and says, "Congratulations! Today, God is giving you His inheritance!"

"Really? Why us?" they reply in astonishment. "We don't deserve anything like that."

But Jesus says, "It's because you fed Me when I was hungry, and when I was thirsty, you gave Me something to drink. You took Me in, gave Me something to wear, and even visited Me when I was in prison."

Still a little surprised, they reply, "You must be thinking of someone else. We did none of those things for You."

But Jesus answers, "You did these things and so much more for so many of My people. You loved those that needed loving. When you did that *for them*, you were doing it *for Me*."

So, in Matthew 25, Jesus essentially charts a course for our lives:

- It's okay to focus on today as long as you don't lose sight of the importance of having a relationship with God. But don't just go through the motions of being religious—your relationship must be genuine.

- Be passionate about developing and applying the talents God has given you to serve others, and whenever you do, He will bless you with new and exciting opportunities.

- God validates and rewards those who use their God-given talents to passionately love Him by showing love toward others.

And there you have it. You can call it what you like: the secret of life, the ultimate answer, or the reason for living. In this book, however, I've commonly referred to it as *our purpose*. Our *real* purpose in life can be summed up in one word—love. You may prefer the term serving, helping, supporting, or guiding, but however you phrase it, it's what we do when we show love for others and put someone else's needs before our own.

For some of you, this may come across as less than revelational. Because deep down, you probably already knew the answer. I'll be completely honest—I knew the answer, too, but not in a way that changed my way of life. You see, ever since I was a boy, I've been told that as a Christian, I'm supposed to love everybody. I don't have to like them, but I have to love them. I was also taught to praise, honor, and love God. But I didn't completely understand how or why it mattered all that much.

However, that all changed for me when I was at my lowest point in life. I had lost businesses, moved away from my friends, and lost my father, job, and church home. My relationship with my wife and sons was strained to the breaking point. I often asked my friends sarcastically, "Could anything else possibly go wrong with my life?"

I kept trying to pick myself up. But I was overwhelmed with a sense of hopelessness. Whenever I tried to explain it to my friends or family, it was clear that no one truly understood what I was going through. I felt isolated. I repeatedly asked God, "Why am I here? Why have you allowed this to happen? Why won't you save me from the mess?" But He didn't come to my rescue, and things continued to get worse.

Then, early one morning, after hundreds of sleepless nights, I cried out to God, "What is it you want me to do?" Now, I ask God questions almost every day, and I believe He answers my prayers in many different ways. But what I'm about to tell you may make you label me as crazy or even worse. You see, believe it or not, I've actually heard God speak to me on a few occasions. That morning was one of those rare moments, and I'll never forget it.

I was lying in bed, trying not to move because I didn't want to wake Pam up. I'd been awake for three or four hours, wishing I could fall asleep. As usual, though, I was consumed with my struggles and praying to God for answers.

"What is it you want me to do?" I whispered aloud.

And this time, He answered me. "Love people."

I was startled, of course, but once the initial shock wore off, I pressed God for more. "I know that. But *how?*" I asked louder, no longer concerned about waking Pam, "How am I supposed to love people?

But there was no answer this time. I guess God had said all I needed to hear—*love people*. So, I got up and sat in what we affectionately call the *big chair* in our bedroom. As I tried to let what had just happened sink in, I sat there whispering the words to myself, "Love people."

God may have different plans for each of us, but we all have the same purpose—to love God by loving others. That makes sense, doesn't it? Deep down inside, I think most of us realize the thing that should matter most in life is serving others.

Still, too many of us leave out one more part of the equation. In the next chapter, we'll look at this final piece of the puzzle Jesus included in His summary of what's most important. Some people are good at it. Maybe a little too good. While others question whether or not it's right or wrong.

CHAPTER 17

Don't Step in #2 While Taking Care of #1

No one's opinion about you matters more than God's.

When you look in the mirror, what do you think about the person staring back at you? If your answer is "Not much," you're not alone. According to Psychology Today Magazine, roughly 85% of people worldwide (adults and adolescents) have low self-esteem. But hopefully, after reading the previous section, you feel more positive about yourself. After all, God thinks so highly of you he has filled your talent bowl full of valuable gifts and talents, and let's face it, no one's opinion about you matters more than God's.

We're so hard on ourselves because we focus on the past and present. But when God looks at us, He sees our entire lives all at once—everything we've ever accomplished and everything we've yet to achieve. So God sees value when he looks at you because He knows your potential and the significance of what He has in store for your life.

Remember, in Matthew 22:39, Jesus said to love others as you love yourself. But what if you don't love yourself? There have been many times when I didn't even like myself. I didn't feel worthy of being loved and hated who I was. I said it like this, "I hate my life." What I was saying was I hated myself for making the choices that had gotten me off course.

So, what does it mean to *love yourself*? There's enough depth in the answer to that question to fill an entire library, and that's precisely why bookstores have "Self Help" sections. But I'd like to tell you what I think. Because I believe this is another instance where we can gain wisdom and understanding by looking at the parent/child relationship.

There's nothing unique about me wanting my sons to love who they are. So it breaks my heart when I see them beating themselves up. Now, if they were to ask me what I think they should be doing to love themselves, I'd make them a list that looks something like this:

- Seek wisdom, and by that, I mean read the Bible and get lots of advice so you make sound choices that bring a secure future.
- Take care of yourself, and by that, I mean don't neglect your health; exercise, eat smart, get plenty of rest, and start doing these things sooner rather than later.
- Do what makes you happy, and by that, I mean find a job or occupation you enjoy, with people you like to be around, and in a place you love.

- Always be learning new things, and by that, I mean to be passionate about gaining knowledge and learning new skills.

- Don't try to be something you're not, and by that, I mean embrace how God made you physically and mentally, and don't worry about what others think.

- Choose your friends wisely, and by that, I mean avoid negative influences. Spend time with positive people who encourage you to become a better person, and this goes for the things you watch and read as well.

- Take pride in yourself and your possessions, and by that, I mean always keep yourself, your home, and your possessions neat, clean, and organized.

- Take time to smell the roses, and by that, I mean spend time enjoying the magical moments God places in front of you every day—like listening to a funny story told by a stranger, watching a flock of birds flying chaotically across the sky, playing air guitar to a song you've not heard in years, getting lost in a painting on your doctor's office wall, closing your eyes and soaking up a moment of sunshine on a chilly day, or sitting alone listening to God's still small voice.

So what do you think? Doesn't that sound like something you might share with a younger person who wasn't sure how to love themselves? Well, you know what? If you were to ask God what you should do to love yourself, I think He'd say something very similar.

I have a business partner with whom I've worked for many years, and he and I have similar tastes in movies. I remember discovering our mutual fondness for the movie I mentioned in the last chapter, *City Slickers*. In one scene, Billy Crystal and his two friends are riding horses, enjoying their time together driving cattle, when they begin to play a game.

"Describe your best day," one of the friends urges Crystal. Then, one by one, each takes a turn to describe the best day of their lives.

For years, at the end of our workday, I would say to my business partner, *"You know, I don't think today was my best day. Maybe tomorrow."*

Several years ago, a counselor asked me to do a similar exercise. It reminded me of that scene from City Slickers. But it was what I would call the deluxe version of "Describe Your Best Day." She asked me to think about what I wanted my life to look like and to put it down on paper. This is my favorite kind of test—one with no wrong answers, and I'm guaranteed to pass. The next day, I scribbled out a list of things my *Best Life* would include. Here's what I wrote:

- Fly fishing (Fishing was at the top of my list. No surprise there.)
- Exploring new places
- Exploring business opportunities
- Consulting business leaders
- Serving others in need
- Spending time with Pamela
- Preparing my sons for life
- Enjoyable physical exercise

I don't know about you, but I'm a goal-setter. So I make a lot of lists. Still, I had never taken the time to make a list like this before, and frankly, I love it. Even today, as I look over this list, I feel alive just thinking about doing these things. Sure, I don't get to enjoy them all every day, but that's because this is my *Best Life List,* and not my *Best Day List.*

You may not have noticed, but half of the items on my list are self-serving, while the other half are more focused on serving others. But regardless of whether they are self-serving or selfish, everything on my list requires life's most valuable commodity—time. And finding time to love others, let alone yourself, can be elusive. That's why in the final section of this book, we'll be looking at some time management tips where you'll hear words like *margin* and *routine.* But that's for later.

Oh, and by the way, there's a place to write down what your *Best Life* would look like in the *Applications* section at the back of this book. But I want to encourage you to hold off until you've finished reading the remainder of the chapters because it might influence which items make your list.

So, what's the moral of the story here? Well, you know how on commercial airline flights, the crew gives their little safety talk, saying, "In the unlikely event of a sudden loss of cabin pressure, oxygen masks will drop down from the panel above your head?" They always emphasize that you secure your mask before helping others. Why? Because if you pass out from a lack of oxygen, you can't help your kids with their masks.

My point is Jesus recognized what so many of us often overlook. Others need our help, but if we don't take care of ourselves, we're no good to anyone.

CHAPTER 18

———

Matthew and the Hurricane

Passion is the fuel needed to fulfill your purpose.

We hoped the day would never come, but a few years after moving to Florida, Pam and I experienced our first hurricane—Hurricane Matthew. In preparation, we bought a stupid-expensive generator, three five-gallon jugs of gasoline, a two-week supply of everything you can imagine, topped off our vehicles with gas, filled up two dozen sandbags, and prepared for the worst. Not knowing what an actual hurricane would be like, we were excited yet anxious as we stayed glued to the TV, watching the storm's latest track.

Our neighbors are phenomenal people. It's one of our favorite things about where we live. They're always so thoughtful and interactive. Pam and I travel a lot. But we never worry about our home because we know they'll keep an eye on things for us while we're gone. However, in the days leading up to the storm, I could sense something was different, and it wasn't just my neighbors.

As the hurricane approached, our entire community was preparing for the storm. People didn't talk about football, work, or school activities. Schools were closed, and so were most businesses. Sporting events, concerts, you name it—they were all canceled. At the grocery store, there wasn't the usual soccer mom chit-chat. Instead, people just nodded and smiled nervously. It was as if everyone was deep in thought, trying to remember if they had forgotten something.

As Hurricane Matthew was producing a torrential downpour outside, I was inside the shelter of our home, studying the book of Matthew and working on the material you are now reading. As I was doing so, I couldn't help but reflect on the passion I had witnessed leading up to the storm.

However, a week later, things had returned to normal for most folks living in our hometown of St. Augustine. We live far enough inland that our home didn't receive any damage from the storm. So, for the folks in our neighborhood, all those tasks we had suddenly become so passionate about just days before were now behind us. Nevertheless, thousands of homes were still without power, and many were no longer habitable. For those unfortunate folks, their passions had shifted from preparing and protecting to surviving and rebuilding.

The word passion comes from the Latin passio and passionem, which means suffering or enduring. For Christians, this word, *passion,* is synonymous with Jesus' entrance into Jerusalem, arrest, subsequent beating, crucifixion, and resurrection. Jesus' purpose was the same as ours: to love God by loving others. He endured unimaginable physical and mental suffering, and often, that's what people do when they're deeply passionate about something.

Today, however, we don't typically associate passion with suffering. In fact, passion is defined as "a strong and barely controllable emotion" or "an intense desire or enthusiasm for something." I believe it's often the deciding factor between enthusiastically living life or merely enduring it.

So let me ask you a question. Is there something you enjoy doing so much you often lose track of time, and hours feel like minutes? Is there anything you're so enthusiastic about you find yourself rambling on and on to others about it? If so, it's most likely something you are passionate about.

Passion is one of those things in life that's hard to measure, not unlike measuring the depth of our love for someone or how happy we are in life. Nevertheless, passion is often the fuel needed to fulfill your purpose. It's what it takes to overcome the hurdles that sometimes get in the way of accomplishing something significant—hurdles like being too busy or being afraid of failing. In other words, the excuses we come up with that God labels as *wicked and lazy*.

Sometimes, I catch myself daydreaming about being great at things. It's pretty bad. Like Ralphie in *A Christmas Story* bad, and truthfully, my daydreams aren't typically about serving others. Most of the time, they're the kind that ends up with me getting pats on the back with ticker-tape parades and people carrying me on their shoulders. Nevertheless, I think it's only natural to long to be great at something.

I once watched a guitar instructor on YouTube describe passion. I wish I could remember his name to give him credit. His description went something like this:

"First comes the opportunity to experience something new. You're interested in trying this new thing. If you enjoy it and are interested enough, you might set aside some time to try it again. Then, if the desire remains, you challenge yourself—striving to improve. You can become *good* by having enough interest to practice the skills and improve your ability. But, to be *great*, you have to move beyond being interested and practicing. To be great, you have to have passion. You no longer try to set aside time to practice; you become consumed with finding time to learn more and grow."

Wow! He was merely talking about playing the guitar, but isn't it true for so many other things in life? What causes us to become passionate about something? I would argue it begins with a conscious decision to be great. We may not get to choose our natural talents, spiritual gifts, and personality traits. But we most certainly choose the things we're passionate about. Let me explain.

We've all experienced a new mother who goes on and on about how her little Sally is off the charts, reading way above her age level, outperforming the other kids, etc. This mother is passionate about raising her daughter and most likely will be for decades. Nevertheless, the degree of her passion may ebb and flow over the years. That's because, even in something innate like parenting, the passion required to be great is still a choice.

Passion is almost always a choice. The mother could choose not to be enthusiastic about her child's progress and selfishly put her own needs before those of her child. Unfortunately, at various levels, neglect happens every day in America and across the globe. Remember, one of the definitions of passion is "a strong and barely controllable emotion." It doesn't say they're "uncontrollable." There's still a choice involved, and every choice has consequences that impact our lives and those around us.

Even when fulfilling our purpose, we can fall short of being who God made us to be. That's because there are varying degrees of passion and sometimes conflicting motivations for why we make choices. Ultimately, though, if you want to live a life of significance, you have to become intentionally passionate about the things God has created you to accomplish. It's what it takes to overcome the hurdles that too often try to keep us from discovering what God has in store for us.

One of my favorite things in life is walking up the middle of a stream or river with a fly rod in my hand. I love being out in nature and trying to outsmart the various species of trout. You might even say I'm passionate about it. In the following chapter, I want us to look at what happens when the things we are passionate about don't align with God's plan for our lives. To do this, I will share yet another embarrassing story about myself.

CHAPTER 19

Teach a Man to Fish and His Wife Will Never See Him Again

It's not easy to know the difference between what's bad for us versus an opportunity that will stretch us in a positive way.

My sons, Andrew and Isaac, are five years apart in age. Five years before Andrew graduated high school, I came up with an idea to take Andrew on a fishing trip each spring, just him and me. Once he left for college, I would start the annual tradition with Isaac, giving both boys five fishing trips with their dad before graduating high school. In my mind, it was a perfect plan. But as Robert Burns once wrote, "The best-laid plans of mice and men often go awry."

The first year, Andrew and I went fishing off Florida's Atlantic coast—the kind of fishing I affectionately call "Deep-Sea Puking." And even though I spent more time lying down than fishing, we had a great time. Andrew even caught two sharks. How cool is that? While driving home from Florida, I asked Andrew if he knew what he'd like to do for our trip the following spring.

"I think I'd like to try fly-fishing," he said. I was a bit surprised. Neither of us had ever picked up a fly rod. A year later, however, we hooked up with an outfitter in picturesque Helen, Georgia. On that crisp February morning, Andrew and I experienced the first of what would become dozens of family fly-fishing trips to the Blue Ridge Mountains in search of an imaginary monster trout we affectionately called Walter.

Andrew enjoyed his first attempt at the art of fly fishing. Our guide, Rex, focused most of his time on my fourteen-year-old, giving him pointers on his casting techniques. Then, without warning, I heard Rex yell, "Let him run, Andrew!"

I watched in astonishment as Andrew fought a hog of a trout for over half an hour. Once he set the hook in the trout's lip, Andrew and Rex hiked about the length of a football field down the middle of the creek to avoid Andrew's line from breaking while the fish wore itself out.

The Rainbow finally tired, and Rex was able to net it. New to fly fishing, I found it hard to believe we were about to let a fish go, especially one big enough to feed my entire extended family twice over. Rex helped Andrew hold the trophy trout while I took a picture. Another angler, who had heard the commotion, came over to witness the catch. Recognizing the significance of the father-son moment, he whispered to me, "That's what it's all about right there."

What none of us realized at that moment, however, was that the fish wasn't the only thing that got hooked that day. Over the next three years, I became more than passionate about fly fishing—I became obsessed. I drove to rivers and streams all over eastern Tennessee and sat watching and waiting until the folks fishing called it a day. Then, I'd stop them, ask about their techniques, and put into practice any tips they had to offer. I bought books, watched videos, and practiced casting in my backyard.

Of course, spending time on a hobby like fishing is a much healthier way to kill time than binge-watching Netflix or playing video games into the wee hours of the morning. Besides, standing in twelve inches of water with a fly rod in your hand is much less stressful than running a business. And weren't some of Jesus' closest friends fishermen? Oh, come on, that was a little funny. Please tell me you at least chuckled.

Seriously though, my workload was keeping me from my family enough as it was. So, when I became passionate about fly fishing, things got really out of whack. But at the time, I was so obsessed I didn't care. I was blinded to any possible negative consequences. Occasionally, I would do the fatherly thing and take my boys with me, but fly-fishing is not a team sport. Most of the time, I went by myself, and I went every chance I could, for hours or even days at a time.

No matter how I tried to justify it, I had fallen into what I call a *pitfall passion*, and falling into a pit is never a good thing. I had a plan, and it was a good plan. But my selfish passion derailed my plans of one-on-one adventures with my sons.

As we discussed in the previous chapters, our passions are choices, and they're derived from "a barely controllable emotion or intense desire." So, we may not even realize a conscious decision was involved. That means that if you're passionate about something that's unhealthy for you emotionally, physically, or spiritually, you may not recognize there's a problem, and that's where it can get dangerous.

Passions come in all shapes and sizes. It's not always easy to know the difference between what's truly bad for us versus an opportunity that will stretch us and bring about growth in a positive way. But of course, some passions will never stand a chance of being a positive part of our lives and should be avoided at all costs. Many of these fall into the category of vices—something that negatively controls us mentally or physically. I can personally relate to someone struggling to overcome a vice. I have an addictive personality, and I've struggled to overcome drugs, gambling, and pornography.

When people learn of my sordid past, it's not unusual for them to want to know how I *kicked* my bad habits. They'll ask, "How did you overcome your addictions?" My response is, "You mean, how *do* I overcome my addictions—present tense." My addictive personality doesn't seem to want to go away. So, my addictions merely change in form and fashion. I have the propensity to get addicted to almost anything.

I once asked my wife to describe me in a single word. Without hesitation, she said, "Workaholic." Ouch. She didn't even have to think about it. I was hoping for something a little more honoring, you know, like handsome, thoughtful, or resourceful. Of course, being addicted to work may be less dangerous than an addiction to drugs or gambling. But still, whether it's drugs, food, golf, fly-fishing, television, video games, or work (these are all things I've struggled with in the past), anything that keeps you from being who God made you to be must be kept in check or avoided altogether. The Bible calls it "idolatry." It's essentially when we allow something to become more important to us than our relationship with God.

So, why do I work so much? I won't lie. I enjoy working. When I help businesses solve problems, I'm working *in* my talents as a leader and administrator. But I have to make sure I don't get out of alignment. Over the years, I've often chosen work over family, with little or no guilt. And for a long time, I didn't understand why it was such an easy choice.

But today, I understand it was because I received more honor at work from employees and customers than from my family. At home, I felt like Rodney Dangerfield—*I got no respect*. But at work, people looked up to me (honor), they told me I had good ideas (praise), and they appreciated my efforts (love). In short, they validated my life. I had no idea if I was making the right choices as a husband and a father at home, and it scared me, so I stayed at work where I felt safe.

I believe God takes pleasure in watching me enjoy healthy activities like fishing. But it's not my purpose. Neither is hunting, playing sports, shopping, streaming TV series, or scrolling through social media. On the surface, there's nothing wrong with any of these things. But when pursued with passion, they have the potential to be as destructive as drugs, alcohol, gambling, or any of the other things we use to escape from our fears and insecurities. Whether it's a vice or a life-consuming bad habit, they can all become pitfall passions.

Speaking of fears and insecurities, in this upcoming section called *Fear to Faithfulness,* we'll discuss how to trade our self-limiting beliefs for unshakeable faith. Faith that we have what it takes to be like the five-talent servant.

PART IV
Fear to Faithfulness

CHAPTER 20

It's a Wonderful, Slightly Terrifying Life

The number one thing that stands in the way of you
fulfilling your purpose in life is not a lack of aptitude,
or knowledge, or even talent—it's fear.

B y all appearances, I was a modern-day George Bailey from the movie *It's a Wonderful Life.* I was a successful business owner, respected in my community, and even asked to serve on nonprofit boards and committees. To onlookers, my marriage and family life seemed far above average. I had several "best friends" who supported and encouraged me. But, I was at that age where, stereotypically, men began questioning their place in life, and as the saying goes, "the grass is always greener on the other side."

I felt like I deserved more in life. I worked harder than anyone I knew, yet I didn't have the spoils to show for it. I used the word *someday* much too often when describing my life, and it began to bother me. To justify my delayed gratification, I wore "busyness" like a badge of honor, trying to impress anyone willing to notice. This apparent midlife crisis didn't find me pining for a sports car, a trophy wife, or skinny jeans. I guess I'm too entrepreneurial for all that. Instead, I wanted financial success and the power that came with it. I used to brag to my friends, "Why would you want to buy a new house when you can buy a new business?"

I hate to admit it, but I even questioned if I *deserved* a better wife—perhaps one who respected my hard work rather than complaining about how little time I spent at home. But Pam didn't seem to notice my frustrations. Instead, she was busy doing what Pam does best, happily caring for those who need her, like our boys and her students. Obviously, there's nothing wrong with that. Still, it made me jealous, and I was too proud to admit it. So, I pretended I didn't want or need her attention.

In retrospect, I wasn't home enough for Pam to realize how much I longed for her approval. The respect I received from my employees, customers, and peers far outweighed any degree of honor my family had to offer. So, I spent most of my time where people validated me. Being a workaholic was clearly problematic, but it was merely a symptom of the actual underlying problem—my insecurity. Today, it's easy for me to see just how close I was to destroying my *wonderful life.*

In his final years of life, my grandfather, Akie, began mentoring me in real estate investing. Along the way, he let me in on many secrets about his business and personal life. This humble, uneducated man was a self-made deca-millionaire who started his entrepreneurial quest soon after his stint as a foot soldier in World War II. He had started from nothing and was the proverbial self-made man. So, you can probably understand how surprised I was to learn a successful, well-respected businessman in his seventies was consumed with insecurity.

Akie was afraid of being taken advantage of, so he was afraid to expand his business. Because he was afraid of losing everything he had worked so hard for, he was afraid to retire. But mainly, Akie was afraid someone would find out how afraid he was. A lot of people looked up to him and depended on him. He once told me, "People think because I've made some money, I know what I'm doing, but I'm just learning as I go like everybody else." For the record, my grandfather was the most remarkable man I've ever known.

Shortly after Akie passed away, an evangelist and friend named Joe McGee happened to be in town speaking at our church. I invited Joe to breakfast and shared with him all the things I'd learned from my grandfather. I explained how Akie's insecurities allowed me to recognize my own for the first time. You see, inside, I felt like a lost little kid who was merely pretending to be an adult, and the thought of someone figuring out I didn't know what the heck I was doing terrified me. Today, this type of thinking is often called *imposter syndrome.*

"I feel like a fraud," I confessed to Joe. "My employees, friends, and even my wife think I've got it all figured out. But in reality, I'm just like my grandfather. It feels like a full-time job trying to hide my insecurities. Will I ever get to a place where I don't feel like this, where I feel like a grown man?"

Joe smiled a patronizing smile and asked me, "Kevin, did you have a birthday recently?"

"Yeah, I did." I answered with a puzzled look, "I just turned 40. Why?"

"You're afraid you're going to die," he said while blowing on his coffee.

"I...don't...think...so," I said, pausing between each word, wondering if he might be right.

Joe concluded my impromptu philosophy class that morning with one last bit of wisdom, "I hate to tell you this, Kevin, but it gets worse. Just wait till you hit 50."

Well, as usual, Joe was right. Now, I wasn't afraid I was about to die, nor was I worried about the pain and suffering that sometimes accompanies it. But as Wayne Dyer puts it, I was afraid of dying with the music still in me. Even though I lived a life envied by those around me, deep down, I saw my life as insignificant. I longed to be a part of something bigger than myself, and I was afraid I might run out of time before I figured out what that something was. As it turns out, I didn't have to wait until I "hit 50" before things got worse. When my dad died, I was 47. He was only 67. His death amplified my fears, and I began asking myself, "What if I only have 20 years left to live?"

So why do I share this story with you? Because time is short, and fear can be paralyzing. The number one thing that stands in the way of you fulfilling your purpose in life is not a lack of aptitude, or knowledge, or even talent—it's fear. People react to fear in many different ways. Fear can stop us dead in our tracks. Fear can keep us from making sound decisions. Fear can lead us to selfish and unhealthy habits or, worse, life-consuming vices and addictions.

Each year, Chapman University conducts the "Survey of American Fears." Have you ever heard it said that public speaking is the thing people are most afraid of?

Well, according to a recent Chapman survey, the fear of speaking in public ranks 32nd on the list. Believe it or not, the survey showed that corrupt politicians are the number one fear of Americans. Of course, more commonplace phobias like being afraid of the dark, heights, spiders, and snakes were toward the top of the list, but that's not the kind of fear I'm talking about.

Whether or not you're willing to admit it, everyone is either afraid or at least dislikes things like failing, being alone, facing change, taking risks, being rejected, etc.

Fear can affect every area of your life and rob you of peace. The Bible calls it a *spirit of fear*. But if, instead, we focus on acquiring knowledge, wisdom, and understanding, we can squash fear and restore our peace. That's precisely why it's so important to understand *who* God wants you to be. So you no longer feel the need to question *why* He made you the way you are.

The Bible has a lot to say about wisdom. It tells us that wisdom is the principal or most important thing (Proverbs 4:7). That makes sense, doesn't it?

After all, knowing you're making a wise decision removes doubt about the possibility of adverse results. In other words, our fear of the unknown is replaced with faith in a positive outcome.

So, how do we get this fear-conquering faith? According to the Bible, "…faith comes by hearing, and hearing comes by the word of God" (Romans 10:17).

Therefore, it only stands to reason that we should find out what the Bible says about it if we want to move from fear to faith. So, in these following few chapters, that's precisely what we will do.

CHAPTER 21

—

Wicked, Lazy and Afraid

*Fear is not an acceptable excuse to the God
who gives you everything you need to succeed.*

In Jesus' story of The Parable of the Talents, we're told the master is about to travel to a "far country." So he calls his servants together and gives them "his goods," or talents, to look after. To avoid any possible confusion, I feel somewhat obligated to remind you who the players in this story represent. The master is, of course, God, and the servants represent me and you—God's real-life servants.

Just like the master in the parable, I've had similar conversations with my employees many times before leaving on a trip. My employees know me well enough to understand what's expected of them. I'll say something like, "Hey, look after this for me while I'm gone." When I return, if everything's like I left it, I'm a happy camper. But God's standards are different from our usual earthly standards. We can assume from the comments made by the one-talent man that the servants knew all too well their master wasn't asking them to look after things if it was convenient or when they got around to it.

This explains why the one-talent servant was afraid and had all kinds of excuses when his master returned home from his trip. You can sense he was hoping the master would show him some mercy, even though he knew the day would come when he would have to account for his lack of action. (Don't forget Matthew 25 is in the front of this book should you need to review it.)

The master called the servant wicked and lazy. I remember being taken aback by this scripture when I first read it. *How could God be so mean?* I thought. *The guy buried the talent to protect it, and he returned it safely to his master. Heck, he didn't even get a pat on the back.* But the more I studied, the more I began to understand how fitting the labels of wicked and lazy were.

Because, yes, the one-talent man was lazy. He knew it would've taken extra effort on his part to invest the talent. Burying the talent was literally the least he could do. If the servant had wanted to safeguard the talent, he would have kept it with him at all times or put it in the bank like the master pointed out to him. So, he was indeed lazy.

We, too, can bury our talents and put them at risk. You have to remember that we're not talking about monetary talents. Jesus used the talent as a metaphor to represent our God-given talents. If we're not diligent about doubling our talents, we may miss opportunities to use them all together. Why? Because life changes. Seasons change. Abilities change. And sometimes, when we don't act, opportunities meant for us are taken by others who aren't afraid to take a chance—leaving us with disappointment and regret.

The one-talent servant was also wicked. If he knew the master wanted him to use the talent, then he must have known how disappointed the master would've been had the talent been stolen. Nevertheless, the one-talent man didn't want the responsibility that came with the single talent. So, he buried it. This goes beyond laziness. He saw the responsibility to oversee the talent as a nuisance—an unwanted obligation.

Let me illustrate my point. If you had something of value you didn't need, say a car, and you told your adult child you're going away for a while and want them to look after the car while you're gone, you'd expect them to drive it, right? Especially if they didn't have a car of their own. But if years later, you return to find your car sitting in the backyard, dirty and neglected, with weeds growing up all around it, and the vehicle no longer ran because it hadn't been driven, you'd be disappointed, wouldn't you?

"Hey, why didn't you use my car?" you ask.

"Yeah, about that," they say, realizing how bad it looks. "I was afraid that I might wreck it, and I knew you'd be upset, so I just parked it in the backyard where it would be safe."

"You ingrate!" You scream, trying to control your temper. "I wanted you to use and enjoy it because I love you. Plus, some of your friends don't have cars either. You could have given them rides to work or school. You could've at least started it and drove it around the block once a week, so it didn't sit here deteriorating. Now the tires are rotten, and the motor is locked up."

The master called the one-talent servant wicked and lazy. But just like me, his wicked and lazy actions were merely symptoms of his underlying problem—his insecurity. This insecurity, or fear, is a slap in the face to God. It's like he was saying, "I know my limitations a lot better than you do, God. I was doing just fine before you tried to tell me what my purpose was. I'm barely getting by as it is, and now you think I should help other people with their problems? What about my problems?"

Fear is not an acceptable excuse to the God who gives you everything you need to succeed. As the parable points out, the master gave his goods to the servants according to each servant's ability. In other words, God knows what each of us is capable of accomplishing. Therefore, he not only gives us the opportunities we're best suited for, but He also gives us what we need to succeed—not too much, not too little.

It's Apollo 13 Engineering at play. Each day, God gives us exactly what we need on our "table of stuff" to accomplish His unique plan for our lives. Of course, I can ask God to give me more to work with, but ultimately, God knows what I need each day to make the square peg fit into the round hole. So, I have to figure out how to accomplish the tasks put before me by creatively using what God's given me to work with. When I serve others in this manner, I'm fulfilling my purpose and growing in my ability to embrace future opportunities.

God is obviously capable of giving me more than I need in life. But if He did so, I might lose my dependence on Him and become prideful or selfish. On the other hand, if God gives me too little, I might get frustrated and lose hope. God's job is to provide me with what I need to succeed. My job is to do my best with what I've been given. But that's not all. I also have to overcome any doubts and fear that it's somehow not enough—that *I'm* not enough. As the old saying goes, actions speak louder than words, and when we walk in faith, we're honoring and praising God with our efforts.

It appeared that the one-talent man honored and respected his master on the surface. He showed up at roll call, listened to instructions, and praised his master with his words and outward appearances. But it stopped there. Unfortunately, many Christians today fall into this same way of thinking. They go to church, sing worship songs, pray, listen to sermons, and even read their Bible occasionally. But isn't that the easy part? Isn't that what the one-talent servant did?

When we're afraid to do what God created and equipped us to do, we dishonor Him through our lack of faith. Again, the hard part is overcoming our insecurities, getting out there, and doing what God created us to do.

Now, chances are you're already serving others. But deep down inside, maybe you recognize God created you for more. I hope you're inspired to overcome your fears. Perhaps it's time to get out of your comfort zone and start praising and honoring God by taking on some of those new opportunities you've been conveniently avoiding.

If you're uncertain about God's plan for your future, I want to encourage you to keep pressing through to the end of this book and on to the applications section. Once there, you'll uncover talents you've buried, maybe unintentionally. Now, in full disclosure, it may require digging up some painful memories from your past. But as I think you'll see in the next chapter, sometimes that's what we need most in our talent bowl.

CHAPTER 22

Put Your Behind in Your Past

Life is a cupful of setbacks and an ocean full of opportunities.

It was John Wooden who said, "Five years from now, you're the same person except for the people you've met and the books you've read." Of course, with all the advancements in technology, this saying should also include what you watch or listen to. The point is that other people's insights and attitudes influence us, whether writers, teachers, friends, or family.

Reading books, scrolling through social media, and watching reality TV will most likely alter your choices in life. However, I believe real-life experiences and actual interactions with others have the most significant impact on who we will be five years from now. Similarly, the more time you spend with someone, the more you understand who they are and whether their beliefs and opinions (or yours) are worthwhile. Likewise, the more you experience something and know how it makes you feel, the more it determines whether or not it's something you'd like to include as a part of your future.

When we're "out there," experiencing what God has in store for us, we increase in knowledge, wisdom, and understanding, and therefore, our abilities increase. Sometimes, new experiences are an introduction to our future passions. But not all are planned, and some are not positive. Nevertheless, I'm a firm believer that things happen for a reason.

When my sons were little, we watched the Disney movie *Lion King* about a thousand times. I love the adult humor in this movie, like when the warthog, Pumbaa, says to Simba, the lion king, "It's just like my buddy Timon says, *you've got to put your behind in your past*."

Timon, the meerkat, corrects Pumbaa, "No, no, no, amateur. Lie down before you hurt yourself. It's *you've got to put your past behind you*."

We've all heard it said you shouldn't dwell on the past. The word "dwell" means *to live in*. So, I agree, we shouldn't live in the past. And that's why I love the gaffe Pumbaa makes by saying, "Put your behind in your past." Because when we do so, we're pressing forward. But that doesn't mean we should abandon our past entirely. As I said before, I believe things happen for a reason. The knowledge, wisdom, and understanding gained from our experiences can be valuable items on our "table of stuff," especially regarding who and how we serve.

In John 10:10, the Bible says the thief (or Satan) comes to steal, kill, and destroy. In other words, bad things happen to good people. Why is that? Face it; there are some questions to which no one on earth knows the answers.

I can't imagine anything worse than the tragedy of a parent losing a child. I've witnessed, from a distance, the fallout from such a loss. Depression, loss of businesses, and even marriages are often torn apart when this happens. Similarly, I know several women who've experienced miscarriages, and I have friends who unexpectedly lost their spouses. But as horrible as those things are, I believe life is a cupful of setbacks and an ocean full of opportunities.

So why does God let us go through horrible events in life? I don't know. But I know one thing for sure: extraordinary healing abilities are given to folks like you and me whenever we experience something tragic. Each day, God gives you what you need. Not only to survive but to help others succeed while going through setbacks you've already experienced. People are afraid. Just like you were when you walked through those things and faced the unknown, they have questions and need wisdom from someone with firsthand experience.

In life, experiences, circumstances, and encounters shape who we were, who we are, and who we will be. Some become defining moments, whether positive or negative, and the emotional impact influences our entire outlook on life. For example, my father often said the Army made him who he was. Moreover, his experience as a helicopter pilot in Vietnam *defined* him.

Some things define who I am, as well. Again, some good and some bad. Like being born in the Bible Belt, being married for thirty-plus years, raising two sons, losing my father unexpectedly, closing a business, working a job that made me miserable, writing this book, and countless others. These experiences not only shape who I am but also who I should serve. It's all part of the Apollo 13 Engineering we discussed earlier. Circumstances and experiences are essential items on our "table of stuff" that God expects us to use to fulfill our purpose each day.

While Pam and I were in Utah, I spent a year getting my private pilot's license. On my final required flight, an FAA inspector rode along with me. We flew from Salt Lake International over to the airport in the military town of Tooele. Not surprisingly, the winds coming off the Great Salt Lake can be unpredictable. As I lined up to land, twenty-five-mile-an-hour crosswinds kicked up, making it nearly impossible to hold the Piper Warrior in line with the runway. My heart was racing a million miles per hour, and I couldn't help but wonder if the inspector noticed how nervous I was.

Like always, I lowered my wing flaps to slow my airspeed for landing. But with the added resistance of the crosswinds, the plane slowed too quickly, and the stall alarm started buzzing, warning me I needed to correct my angle of descent. The only thing I needed to do was push forward on the yoke and level out the plane. But I was so worried about what the inspector was thinking that I froze in indecision.

Suddenly, the airplane stalled and dropped like a rock toward the runway a few hundred feet below.

My mind was racing, and I struggled to breathe. I was no longer worried about failing the inspection. The only thing going through my mind was, *I'm about to die.* The inspector waited a few moments to see how I would respond, but my fear paralyzed me. He calmly took control of the plane, leveled us out, and asked if I wanted to try again. I passed my inspection that day, but whenever I piloted flights in the future, there were times when fear would cover me like a blanket, making it difficult to breathe. I was so embarrassed about the panic attacks I didn't tell anyone. I hung up my wings a few months later and haven't piloted a plane since.

I still experience similar attacks—sometimes while scuba diving or in the dentist's chair. I once had an episode during dinner with a prospective client. It seems the older I get, the more often they occur. I hate that my brain controls my body like this. But, for now, it appears to be a part of life. I've pinpointed some of the triggers, and I'm learning to cope. Sometimes, I'm able to avoid them altogether. Nevertheless, these experiences have given me valuable insight. And I recently had a chance to put my *talents* to the test.

While on one of my regular business trips to our company in Tennessee, something unplanned forced me to leave my truck behind and take a commercial flight back to Florida. I offered an employee a bonus to drive my truck to Florida and catch a flight back home. Once he arrived in St. Augustine, we went to Orlando, where I dropped him off at the airport. About 30 minutes later, he called, saying there was a problem, and asked me to return and pick him up. So, I turned around and headed back to the airport.

"Man, I'm really sorry," he said. "I've always had a fear of flying, but I thought I would be okay this time. I guess I was wrong. I freaked out before I even got on the plane."

From a timing and a financial standpoint, this really stunk. If this had happened fifteen years earlier, I would have fired this employee on the spot. But on that day, because of my own experiences, I understood how embarrassed he must have been. So, to put him at ease, I shared with him about my panic attacks. He recognized his lack of forethought had disappointed me, and he shouldn't have taken on the task in the first place. But he also understood he wasn't alone and wouldn't lose his job over it.

The story I just shared is only a tiny example of how God presents us with opportunities to show a little love to others. Carl Sandburg once said, "Nearly all the best things that came to me in life have been unexpected, unplanned by me." If everything happens for a reason, experiences are divine educational opportunities designed to help us help others someday.

The impact of my actions lasted much longer than it took me to carry out God's plan on that day. Most opportunities for servitude are like that. But sometimes, tiny opportunities grow into bigger-than-life causes worth fighting for. And as Sandberg points out, nearly all are unexpected.

But whether or not they catch us off guard, opportunities requiring a commitment should be approached differently than simple random acts of kindness. So, our next chapter breaks down some of the do's and don'ts when you find yourself faced with an opportunity to make a difference in a big way.

CHAPTER 23

Baby Steps and Belly Flops

Timeliness is more important than flawless execution.

The water in the swimming pool looks refreshing. The sun is beating down so fiercely that your skin is glistening with a thin layer of sweat. You bend one leg and swish the opposite foot through the water. *Whoa! That's pretty chilly.* But you know it will be okay once your body adjusts to the temperature. So now, you have two choices—get in a little at a time or all at once.

Most people are too afraid of the shock that comes from diving in headfirst. We don't know how cold it will be with any degree of certainty. Are you more likely to use the steps at the shallow end of the pool, adjusting to the temperature a little at a time? Or are you the type of person who prefers diving in headfirst, subjecting your entire body to the cold all at once, but by doing so, shortening the time needed to adjust to the water temperature?

Most often, our personality determines the preferred method of entering the pool. Peaceful Phlegmatics and Perfect Melancholies will probably choose the stairs. In contrast, Powerful Cholerics and Popular Sanguines are more likely to jump in all at once. These same character traits also determine how we prefer to tackle new challenges in life. Just like getting into the swimming pool, there are two options.

The first is to take baby steps, gaining confidence as you move from getting your feet wet, to wading, then waist deep, etc. The second option is to go all-in. Call it what you want—jumping in with both feet or diving in headfirst. Now, I'll be honest with you, I'm a big chicken. But still, I'm the kind of guy who would yank the Band-Aid off rather than prolong the pain by finessing it loose. Likewise, I prefer to confront challenges and new opportunities head-on, but that doesn't mean I'm brave. I simply want the fear of the unknown to go away as soon as possible. It also doesn't mean I'm smart. Because when it comes to being a servant, there are three potential problems when fully committing in this manner.

The first potential downfall of diving in headfirst when serving others is taking on a role we aren't suited for. Just because someone asks for help or we see an opportunity to serve doesn't mean it's part of God's plan for our lives. Taking on a role outside of your spiritual giftedness may leave your effort to show some compassion looking less like a swan dive and more like a belly flop. Trust me, as someone who tends to leap without looking, it can be ugly. Maybe you've been on the receiving end of this sort of help from some well-meaning individual. You found yourself thinking *I know this person means well, but I would have been better off if I'd never asked for help.*

Another potential downfall of the all-in strategy is what I call *justified procrastination.* This is when we put off starting until we're confident we've got all our ducks in a row and everything is just right. Then, whether jumping into a pool or a new opportunity, we tell ourselves everyone is watching—judging our abilities—even though that's rarely the case.

So, instead of taking action, what do we do? Everything but what actually makes an impact. We spend time planning, preparing, perfecting, and all along the way, we justify our procrastination. Keep in mind we're talking about loving people in need. So, a little hesitation on our part may mean a lot of pain for someone else. When it comes to being a servant, I believe timeliness is more important than flawless execution.

The final potential problem is over-committing. When we take on too many responsibilities and spread ourselves too thin, we risk letting down the folks depending on us. Being overcommitted can also lead to neglecting other essential things in life, including our health, which without, we're of no use to anyone. If you say *yes* to every opportunity that comes along, pretty soon, you'll not have any time left to love on yourself.

As servants, we're kind of like the Blues Brothers: *We're on a mission from God.* So, one might assume that because we're following our divine calling, God will intuitively part the seas of any struggle we face. But in reality, that's nothing more than sanctified ignorance.

God is more than able to get us out of self-induced predicaments we've created. But God is also our heavenly Father, and just like every good earthly parent, He wants us to learn from our missteps because gaining knowledge, wisdom, and understanding from a wrong decision is often more beneficial than miraculously being rescued from it.

Whether you're overcommitted or said "yes" to an opportunity you should have passed on, there's an obvious solution. You've probably already considered it—it's called quitting. But quitting can have severe consequences, including the tendency to become overly protective of our time and immediately saying *no* to anything new.

When we choose to say *no* to an opportunity God has custom-tailored for us, it's like picking up a shovel, heading out into the backyard, and burying our talents. There has to be a better way. Rather than quitting, my advice is to be bold and share your feelings with everyone involved. Try to find some middle ground and maybe set up some boundaries. At a minimum, pull out a calendar and agree upon a date when you'll step down from your commitment. Just be sure and do whatever it takes to finish strong and leave without any emotional baggage.

And this brings up a great point. Maybe it goes without saying, but long-term commitments should not be taken lightly. After all, you're not the only person who suffers when things don't go perfectly. That's why I believe it's healthy to communicate any reservations or limitations you may have *before* committing.

The same is valid on the flip side of that coin as well; make sure you're willing to live up to the expectations of the people you're serving. You might even consider putting things in writing so you can go back and remind yourself what was agreed upon.

Now, if the thought of confronting someone and telling them what you are and are not willing to do freaks you out a little bit, I get it. My wife, Pam, is the same way. But I promise it's better to set boundaries up front and risk someone getting their feelings hurt than getting stuck doing something God didn't intend for you to do.

Speaking of Pam, she is the inspiration for the topic of discussion in our upcoming chapter.

CHAPTER 24

Two-Talent Pam

God is more concerned about our willingness
to try than our level of success.

My wife, Pam, has never been one for goal setting, and she's typically not too keen about getting out of her comfort zone either. She'd prefer to read a fiction novel by John Grisham than a personal development book by John Maxwell. Now, don't get me wrong, she's one of the most selfless people you could ever meet. I constantly have to beg Pam to put her needs before mine, our sons, and even her students. I do not doubt that God looks down on my wife and says, "Well done." Maybe that explains why she's never been overly concerned about receiving affirmation from others. Pam was and is a better human than I'll ever be.

But still, her lack of drive, at least in comparison to mine, concerned me. While I was striving to become a "five-talent servant," Pam, for the most part, seemed content with life. Her apparent complacency made me question whether God saw her as a one-talent or two-talent person. But, of course, you have to remember that I thought the parable was mainly about making money back then. So, I continually encouraged Pam to return to college and become a school administrator or maybe leave academia and start a business. The way I saw it, being satisfied with where you were in life wasn't acceptable.

Pam was afraid she might not have what it takes to move up in her career, and her fear caused me to question her "ranking" in the eyes of the Big Man upstairs. Nevertheless, Pam was happy simply focusing on her three passions in life—her family, her students, and her relationship with God. I wanted my wife to be happy—you know what they say—happy wife, happy life. But I didn't want God labeling her as wicked and lazy, either. Meanwhile, all this pondering led me to an even bigger question: *If God sees someone as a two-talent person, is it okay for that person to be content in life, or does He expect us to strive to be more like the five-talent servant who his master showed additional favor?*

If you don't remember what I'm referring to, both the two-talent and five-talent servants doubled their talents and were validated equally by their master. However, what confused me was that the master ordered that the single talent taken from the one-talent servant be given to the five-talent servant.

This was completely counterintuitive to my way of thinking as a business manager. In my opinion, the two-talent servant was the obvious choice to oversee the one additional talent. Why? Because he had a lot less on his plate, 150% less, in fact. Plus, I'm a competitive guy, and if I were the two-talent servant in the parable, I would have wanted a means to catch up to my five-talent peer. So it seemed unfair to me that the master, who represents God, would give the extra talent to the five-talent servant, who still had more than double that of his coworker.

Of course, you can't forget that even though the talents in the parable were monetary, Jesus was only using talents as a metaphor. With this in mind, it's easier to understand the master's decision to give the additional responsibility to the five-talent servant. Let me explain why.

Pretend you were in need for a moment, and God wanted me to help you. But like the one-talent man, I was afraid I wasn't up for the responsibility. So, I buried my talent deep within myself and ran from the opportunity, potentially leaving you in a place of desperation. If you were suffering and needed help, would you want God to send just anyone available? Or would you want Him to give the assignment to someone with a track record of getting things done?

I can picture God telling His angels something like, "This is too important to risk. This person has already been let down once. I better send someone more qualified, so take the talent from the servant who was afraid and give it to the servant who now has ten talents. I *know* he won't let us down."

We see this same principle play out all the time in the business world today and pretty much in all walks of life. People who are dependable and show they're not afraid to take on more responsibility are typically asked to do just that. At the same time, responsibilities and opportunities are taken away from those who mismanage, underperform, or merely flake out. This is why the parable goes on to say:

> 29 *'For to everyone who has, more will be given, and he will have abundance; but from him who does not have, even what he has will be taken away.'*
> *Matthew 25:29 New King James Version (NKJV)*

You see, the five-talent man had something the others didn't. Maybe he was more experienced, more knowledgeable, or had more faith. But whatever it was, I wanted it. Something inside me longed for that same sort of favor, or as the parable called it, abundance. Admittedly, greed most likely played a big part in my desires. Still, the way I saw it, this was a divine mandate to double my financial holdings. If God was going to hand out financial opportunities to whoever was willing to take on more risk and responsibility, it might as well be me.

Now, I understand I'm taking some liberties by suggesting the five-talent servant was somehow better than the two-talent servant. After all, they both doubled what was given to them and were validated equally by their master. But still, the five-talent man was shown additional favor, and this wasn't the first time either. Right out of the gate, he was given more talents than his two counterparts.

And that brings us back to the question at hand: *Is it okay to be content as a two-talent servant, or does God expect us to strive to be like the five-talent man?* You know, someone who is willing to take on more responsibility. This is actually a two-part question, but the short answer to both is *yes*. Of course, God wants us to be all we can be—to double our talents and significantly impact those around us. But for many folks, there are seasons of serving, so consuming it requires pressing the pause button on any new opportunities or invitations to serve.

Right about now, you may be thinking, "Man, Kevin sure is reading a lot into this. How can he be so sure?" And that's a great question. Because I wasn't sure for a very long time. But then, one day, all of a sudden, it hit me. You see, the parable could have easily been about only two servants, the one-talent man who was afraid and the five-talent man who was validated. But instead, Jesus included a third servant in his story. And as with all of Jesus' parables, something can be learned from every plot and every player. So, the role of the two-talent servant requires careful consideration.

As I've pointed out repeatedly, the master was equally pleased with the efforts of both the two-talent *and* five-talent servants. He didn't say, "Good job, number two, but I wish you could be more like number five." No. He said, *Well done.* So why didn't the master give that additional talent to the two-talent servant, and why, at the beginning of the story, was one servant given more talents than the other two put together? We don't know exactly, but we do know that the Bible tells us the amount each man was given to oversee was done according to his ability.

Maybe the two-talent man wasn't as experienced or educated, or his physical and mental abilities weren't equal to that of the five-talent servant. Perhaps it was because the two-talent man was already in a season of serving that required a high degree of focus—something like caring for an aging parent or a child with special needs.

When I was younger, I spent a week each summer working as a camp counselor for the Muscular Dystrophy Association. I was only a teenager, but when my week of caring for my *camper* was over, I can remember wondering how on earth his parents managed the other 51 weeks out of the year. My point is that the master, who represents God, understood that the two-talent servant didn't need the additional responsibility. He was right where God wanted him to be at that time.

So I think it's clear that even though God expects us to double our talents, sometimes, if we're loving on who God needs us to be loving on, it's okay to be content. But I also believe we mustn't allow our contentment to shift over into an attitude of complacency. Contentment is defined as *a state of peaceful happiness* and focuses more on the present. While complacency, defined as *a satisfaction of one's achievements*, focuses on past accomplishments.

I don't know about you, but when I'm doing something impactful and folks start praising me, I tend to coast rather than finish strong, and that's not good. Because I truly believe the difference between hearing God say "well done" or calling you out as "wicked and lazy" lies somewhere in the gray area that separates contentment and complacency.

That said, let's circle back to the beginning of this chapter and my concerns about my wonderful wife Pam being a one-talent servant. Because still to this day, there are times when opportunities come her way, and she allows her fears to get the best of her, and she buries her talents like the one-talent man. Even though they align with her spiritual gifts of compassion, serving, and encouraging.

But there are other areas of her life where it's easy to see she's more like the two-talent servant. Because she consistently shows up over and over without complaining or getting burned out and quitting. You can sense that she's genuinely grateful for the opportunity to honor God with her talents.

And then there are also times when I watch my wife step boldly out of her comfort zone and take on something that honestly makes me a little afraid. I'll usually give her a look, letting her know I'm worried about her. But she does this thing where she takes a long, deep breath and glances my way without turning her head. Then she smiles and gives me a wink, letting me know it's okay and not to worry. I can't help but shake my head and chuckle because I know there's no stopping her at that point.

These are the moments when my wife is like the five-talent servant, even though I can tell she's not exactly sure how things will turn out. I guess her faith overcomes her fear somehow because she just puts one foot in front of the other and goes for it. And that's so cool because I believe God is more concerned about our willingness to try than our level of success. God understands that often what we label as a failure is instead an exercise in faith and a lesson on how to love others more effectively.

So yes, sometimes my wife *is* a one-talent servant, but there are also seasons in her life where there's no doubt she's like the two-talent servant. And still, there are times when it's easy to recognize that Pam is a five-talent servant. Heck, maybe even a fifty-talent servant. But you know what? The same is true for you and me.

When you look into your past, it's probably not too hard to pinpoint some "one-talent moments" when fear kept you standing on the sideline. I'm right there with you—guilty as charged. But I'm also guessing there were times when you've made sacrifices that greatly impacted others. Even if you didn't understand the servant's role you were playing at the time. Maybe you're still making those sacrifices.

Whether these opportunities to serve feel like "two-talent," "five-talent," or "fifty-talent sacrifices," they all require replacing our fear with what I call "five-talent faith."

CHAPTER 25

———

Five-Talent Faith

Many times, the real measure of success is whether we're giving it our all or merely going through the motions.

I n the past, I've enjoyed watching a TV show called *The Amazing Race,* where people in teams of two compete by racing to exotic cities all over the world. At many of the destinations, the teams must complete a physical or mental challenge called a "Detour." Once they've completed the challenge, they begin the next leg of their race to a new destination, and so on, until they reach the finish line.

But the successful completion of each Detour is typically subjective, with a judge deciding if the team has completed the challenge well enough to move on to the next leg of the race. If a team cheats or doesn't finish their challenge satisfactorily, they must start all over. Only after receiving "validation" from the judge for a job well done do they find out what destination they will race to next, and again, that's just the destination. What new challenge will they face once they arrive? They have no idea until they get there.

As servants of God, this TV show parallels our own "Amazing Race." There are new opportunities to love others in need at each *destination* or season in life. But often, new opportunities come with unexpected challenges or "Detours." And just like on the TV show, many times, the real measure of success is whether we're giving it our all or merely going through the motions.

I know I keep saying this, but it truly is a matter of the heart. I can sing praises to God all the livelong day and still hear him tell me that I'm wicked and lazy. How? Well, as the old saying goes, "Words are cheap." When we are in a serving capacity, it typically requires a personal sacrifice in some area of our lives. So, I guess that's why we also have the saying, "Actions speak louder than words."

Think about it. Why does God want us to praise and worship Him? Is it because He's full of Himself and needs us to tell him how awesome He is? Hardly. You see, God understands the value of living a life of gratitude. I believe God wants us to serve others because by doing so, we demonstrate our gratitude for everything he's given and done for us.

Case in point, it's nice when my sons tell me they love me. As parents, we long to hear those magic words. But I'd trade it in a heartbeat for an opportunity to see my "mighty men of valor" living out lives of significance by loving God, others, and themselves. That's because their actions let Pam and I know they've embraced what we worked so hard to teach them as parents. The same holds true for our relationship with God. He wants us to love Him with more than mere words.

In The Parable of the Talents, the servants understood this. It was their actions that communicated their honor and respect to their master. But the one-talent man was not only afraid of failing; he was worried about the sacrifice he would have to make to double his single talent.

A side note here: Failing to double our talents doesn't change how much God loves us. When they were growing up, I repeatedly reminded my sons, Andrew and Isaac, that their actions don't change how much I love them. When teaching your child how to do something, you don't expect them to always get it right. You kind of expect them to fail from time to time. But wouldn't you rather they fail and learn than not even try because they're afraid they might disappoint you? Again, the same holds true for our relationship with God.

Initially, I planned on titling this book *The Five-Talent Man*. Not because he had the most talents but because I believe the five-talent man had more faith than the other servants. He was the master's "go-to" servant. He wasn't afraid of the possible sacrifices required to double his talents. The five-talent servant understood his purpose so well he completely trusted the master (God) would always do what was in his best interest. In other words, he didn't ask what the odds of success were or what the cost might be. The five-talent man had faith that he was equipped to succeed, even though he had no idea what was needed to pull it off.

The paragraph below is a prayer. It's the kind of prayer a five-talent servant prays.

Father God, I want people who are hurting to know how much you love them. So, I give you permission to use me today. Please show me who I should serve and how best to love them. Help me hear your instructions clearly and keep me from being too busy or too afraid to use the talents you've given me. Thank you, Father, for giving me everything I need to fulfill my purpose and have an abundant life. Amen.

If you pray this prayer each morning, or one similar to it, I promise your life will change in remarkable ways. But chances are, if you're like most folks, you're kind of afraid to pray a prayer like this because it might require a sacrifice on your part.

Maybe I'm wrong, but I don't think I know a single person who feels their lives aren't already busy enough. So, while you're giving God permission to use you to help others, you might also be thinking that the last thing you need is something else on your plate. My friend, Joe McGee, once said, "If you think your plate's full, you need to get a bigger plate." I'm not 100% sure, but I think that means we must have faith that we can do anything God wants us to do.

But of course, you have to be smart about what you sign up for. I'm the type of person who wants to take on every opportunity that comes my way. I've heard this kind of thinking called the "shiny object syndrome." The problem is overdoing it and taking on too much can lead to mediocrity and missed opportunities. As David Allen so wisely put it, "You can do anything, but you can't do everything." And that's why it's so important to identify your talents and understand *who* God made you to be so you can understand *who* He made you to serve. And perhaps just as importantly, who He did *not* create you to serve.

Can you believe it? It's time for the final section of this book, *Gong Show To Talent Show*. That means you've almost reached the finish line. Unless God's been telling you, it's time to get a bigger plate. If so, you may just be stepping up to the starting line. In any case, in this last section, I will wrap everything up by giving a brief recap and offering up some practical applications. By the time you've completed these final chapters, you'll be ready to move on to the *Applications* section. There, you'll be able to fine-tune God's unique plan and begin charting your course to an abundant life.

PART V
Gong Show to Talent Show

CHAPTER 26

Here Comes the Judge

If you want to be a history maker,
having the heart of a servant is the first step.

n the late 1970s, a television producer named Chuck Barris pitched an idea to the networks for a new TV game show called *The Gong Show*. This sad excuse for an amateur talent show would have never stood a chance of making it past the first stage of consideration on its own merits. However, early in his career, Barris created the wildly popular television show *The Dating Game*, so he had some inroads to gain network approval.

At the time, I was a typical preteen who thought the funniest thing in the world was when my dad told me to pull his finger. So, the crude humor of *The Gong Show* was almost as appealing as my favorite show at that time, *Gilligan's Island*.

On *The Gong Show*, Barris, who was also the host, introduced various talent acts that performed before the studio audience and three celebrity judges. Behind the judge's table hung a large gold gong and a proportionally sized mallet. Each participant had 90 seconds to show off their talent, or lack thereof, after which the judges would score them from 0 to 10. Unfortunately, the performers were often so terrible that a judge would grab the mallet and strike the gong, prematurely ending the competitor's performance.

If you're too young to have experienced *The Gong Show*, trust me, you didn't miss much. But if that's the case, you might be more familiar with a similar, more modern show called *America's Got Talent*. Talent shows like these demonstrate our instinctive longing to be praised and honored.

Over the last four sections, I've taken you on a journey of what I hope has been either one of discovery or confirmation—and perhaps a little of both. As I've said before, I understand how anticlimactic it can seem on the surface to find out your true purpose in life is as simple as serving others. But if that's how you feel, I want to challenge you to look at things differently.

In chapter 10, we explored Jesus' choice of the talent as the monetary measurement given to the servants in The Parable of the Talents. If you'll remember, the talent was a vessel in which valuable commodities were measured. So, I believe God understood the word talent would play an integral role in our modern-day translation of this parable. After all, our unique combination of "talents" makes us valuable and worthy of being part of God's big plan.

Likewise, there is another metaphor to be considered from The Parable of the Talents, and that's Jesus' choice to tell the story using servants as the principal players. He could have chosen infinite storylines using various people from varying backgrounds. However, Jesus chose to use servants to represent you and me in a story demonstrating God's desire for us to love others. And there's no better way to love someone than by serving them.

So again, if discovering your true purpose in life is somewhat less than you had hoped for, I get it. When I first figured it out, that's how I felt as well. I'd dreamed of "saving the world" and "setting the woods on fire"—and I'm not even sure what that means! But it sounds good, doesn't it? It sounds much more exciting than teaching your kids something *on purpose*. Or sharing a meal with a homeless person. Or watching other people's kids during church. Or driving your neighbor to their doctor's appointment. Or organizing a fundraiser for a local nonprofit.

Whether it's a simple random act of kindness or a massive undertaking serving multitudes of people, we'll likely never know how far-reaching our actions truly are. Similarly, we can't fully understand the importance of God's next mission for us, should we choose to accept it.

Remember, the big picture is much greater than our limited minds can comprehend, and that's because we tend to think about serving only those within our arm's reach. But often, momentous accomplishments come about from humble beginnings, and that's because we can't possibly understand the full scope of God's plans. The Bible says, "No eye has seen, no ear has heard, and no mind has imagined what God has prepared for those who love him." (1 Corinthians 2:9, NLT)

A perfect example is the story of Nancy Brinker. Before losing her sister, Susan, to breast cancer, Nancy promised she would fight to end the disease. Even though, at first, she had no idea what to do other than raise money. As Nancy describes it, "I started with $200 and a shoebox full of potential donor names." The story might have ended there, but Nancy's passion was renewed when she, too, was diagnosed with the disease only two years later.

Around that time, running was becoming more and more popular. So, Nancy began organizing races to raise money for cancer research. She then created a nonprofit and sought out worthy researchers to receive grants. Today, the Susan G. Komen Organization is the world's largest nonprofit funding source for the fight against breast cancer. They've invested almost $3 billion into research and related programs in over 60 countries. Maybe you've not heard of the organization. Nevertheless, I'm guessing you've probably seen the pink ribbons they created to bring support and awareness to the cause.

When she made the promise to her sister, Nancy had no plans, only passion. She never dreamed that one day, an organization she named after her sister would be credited for reducing breast cancer cases by more than half. It just goes to show you'll never know what doors God is willing to open until you're willing to walk through them.

So don't be deflated because God's plan for your life isn't as grandiose as you'd hoped. Instead, embrace how easy it is for you to be, not just good, but truly great at something. How predictable it is to make a worldly impact by simply changing the world around you. How important it is for you to share some love with your neighbors who are hungry, hurting, and hopeless. But most of all, just how vital it is to recognize God is longing to validate your efforts and say, "Well done, good and faithful servant."

You see, when you decide to step up on that stage and put your talents to the test, there's no panel of celebrity judges. Well, I guess that's not entirely true. God is famous, but I'm not sure I'd call Him a celebrity. Nevertheless, God is your only true judge, and His vote is the only one that matters. Just remember, He's more concerned about what motivates you than the final score.

Oh, and that big gold gong? It's still there, but it's no longer behind the judge's table. In fact, there is no judge's table. Because God prefers to walk alongside us in case we stumble and need help along the way. That's right; you're the only person who can strike the gong and end the show.

So if you've given up on yourself or think God's given up on you, remember, the great "I am" is a God of unlimited "do-overs." And if you believe God is dead or doesn't care about humanity—put Him to the test. Try praying a "five-talent prayer" every day for a week and see what happens. I promise He'll open up a door of opportunity for you to share some love.

God wants you to be a history-maker. So, get ready to chart a new course because these final chapters will help you develop a plan.

CHAPTER 27

———

Only Fools Rush In

Wisdom is knowing how, when, and why to make a decision.

For some time now, I've been leading you down a rabbit hole of touchy-freely metaphors and overarching concepts without a whole lot of practical application. Nevertheless, I hope my collection of ramblings has been as equally helpful to you as it was for me to put them down on paper. But now, I'd like to shift gears and explore some practical ways you can apply what you've learned. So, what do you say? Are you ready to develop a plan and set a course toward fulfilling your purpose in life? Then, let's get started.

As we learned from The Parable of the Talents, God validates those who "double their talents." So, the logical place to begin is by asking *How does someone double their talents?* I mean, what does that even look like? Especially since measuring something intangible like our talents is difficult at best.

So first, let's summarize what our talents are made up of. I believe the talents God bestows upon us can be divided into three groups:

1. Natural Talents, Spiritual Gifts, and Personality Traits
2. Knowledge, Wisdom, and Understanding
3. Everything Else

Natural Talents, Spiritual Gifts, and Personality Traits

Generally speaking, our natural talents consist of three categories: physical, mental, and creative. Identifying natural talent is usually not that difficult. We often figure this out simply by comparing our abilities to those around us. Sometimes, however, others point them out to us through words of encouragement or validation.

We typically turn to our natural talents when we first begin serving others. Yet, more often than not, they are the least impactful when it comes to fulfilling our purpose in life. That's partly because the responsibilities and obligations of life tend to crowd out the things we were once passionate about in our younger days.

Nevertheless, we can and should hold on to the essence of those natural talents that defined us in the past. Because if you "used to be" athletic, artistic, skilled academically, etc., you probably still are, even though you might not measure up to the latest cream of the crop. So, who knows, maybe it's time to dig up those buried talents from years gone by and ask God to open a door of opportunity. Then, you can embrace your past and use your talents to show a little love and support to others with similar passions.

Next are our spiritual gifts, which, as I've stated before, are by far the most important of our talents. That's because they lie at the heart of where God wants us to be motivated. You see, God understands that our "sweet spot" for living an abundant life comes from embracing our spiritual gifts. So whether God created you to be a perceiver, server, teacher, exhorter, giver, administrator, or someone filled with compassion, become intentional about putting these talents into practice.

When we apply the gifts God has put inside of us, we're more likely to remain passionate, avoid burnout, and become truly great at whatever we choose to do. But, unfortunately, spiritual gifts can be hard to identify. So, if you want to be great at serving others, you'll need to put in the necessary effort required to fully understand what I like to think of as our "supernatural powers."

The final talent in this first group is our personalities or, as they are also commonly referred to, character traits. Most of you would agree that character traits are the least important of our talents. However, serving others almost always involves the complex world of relationships, and let's face it, relationships can get messy. If our purpose were simply to love God and ourselves, it wouldn't matter because we're pretty good at putting up with our own shortcomings. But that's not the case. Our purpose is to love God by loving others.

Identifying and fully understanding our character traits, or the way we're wired, dramatically increases our ability to react positively to situations and circumstances. But even more importantly, by understanding and respecting the personalities of others, we significantly improve how successful and effective we are as servants of God.

Knowledge, Wisdom, and Understanding

You've probably heard the saying, "Life is the best teacher." All of us were born involuntarily into unique circumstances; therefore, we've all had our fair share of unique experiences. Our circumstances and experiences shape us and sometimes define us. But they are unarguably the most significant contributors to our second group of talents—knowledge, wisdom, and understanding.

I like to think of knowledge, wisdom, and understanding as a three-legged stool that will confidently support you. But take away any of the three, and you are left with some uncertainty about your decisions. Let's take knowledge, for example. When we think of knowledge, formal education typically comes to mind. But we all know someone who is "book smart" yet has no common sense. If you had to put your life in the hands of this person, how much confidence would you have in their decision-making abilities?

King Solomon is considered by many as the wisest person ever to have lived. In the book of Proverbs, Solomon tells us that wisdom is the principal, or most important, thing. He goes on to say, "The fear of the Lord is the beginning of wisdom." Remember, *fearing* God doesn't mean being afraid. Instead, it's demonstrating respect, gratitude, honor, praise, and love. So, if you want to grow in wisdom, fearing God is the best place to start.

Most people would define wisdom as knowing the difference between right and wrong. However, the "Kevin McBroom definition" of wisdom is knowing how, when, and why to make a decision.

King Solomon also pointed out that when we get wisdom, we gain understanding, which is pivotal. Because understanding removes doubts and fears and replaces them with confidence and peace. Doubt and fear kept the one-talent servant from becoming who God created him to be. In comparison, the five-talent servant had confidence in his abilities and a spirit of peace that overcame his fears.

Everything Else

So what else is there, you may be asking? This may sound contradictory after reading almost an entire book where I pointed out how stupid I was for thinking God wanted me to double my financial holdings. But still, if your spiritual gift is "giving," it helps to have some resources to give away.

Regardless of our gifts, we all have resources that could be used to improve our ability to serve, and I'm not just talking about money. Things like our homes, vehicles, material possessions, etc., can be used to love others. Even intangible things like influence and the network of people you know can be included as items on your table of stuff. Because, believe it or not, God has blessed you with those things to serve others more effectively. So I think it only makes sense to include them along with the talents we can double.

But you mustn't forget, what makes up *your* talents will never be the same as mine. Likewise, God's plan for *your* life will look very different than mine.

CHAPTER 28

—

Doubling Your Talents

You'll never know what doors God is willing to open until you're willing to walk through them.

Now that we've finished our refresher course on what makes up the items in our talent bowl or, as I like to call it, our table of stuff, we're ready to tackle the subject of doubling our talents. But unfortunately, we have a slight problem because the bulk of our talents can't be measured with any degree of certainty. We can obviously measure the value of our financial resources and material possessions, and there are also methods to measure our physical and mental aptitudes. But beyond this, the bulk of what makes up our talents can't be easily quantified.

But that's okay because I believe doubling our talents is more of a mindset than a discernible metric. It's part of what I've been referring to as "five-talent faith." This is certainly up for debate, but I believe we're doubling our talents anytime we increase in desire and ability to serve others, whatever that looks like.

Now, that doesn't mean we get to be loosey-goosey about it. There's a saying in the military, "When you fail to plan, you plan to fail." So, if you agree with me that loving God by loving others is why God put you on this earth, it only makes sense that you should have a plan.

Getting Started

Odds are, you're already serving others in some form or fashion. How can I be so confident? Because that's just what most people do, at least to some degree. If you merely factor in raising children or helping other family members, it would include most of the human race. Nevertheless, you probably didn't choose your current assignment. Instead, it chose you.

That means there's a good chance you're not serving in an area that aligns with your talents. Now, if that's the case, don't panic. Most of us go through times when we're obligated to serve outside of our talents. But, if you plan on doubling your talents, you'll want to become more intentional about the roles you take on.

Once you've completed the *Applications* at the back of this book, you'll have a pretty good idea of who the people or persons are you should be serving. Then, you can start applying the principles in this book while asking God to help make it happen. Once you've opened your mind to the concept of intentionally serving others, you'll be surprised how quickly God will open doors of opportunity.

Of course, it's not always as straightforward as introducing yourself, rolling up your sleeves, and getting to work. Especially when you're not wired as an extrovert. So, for many, getting involved with a nonprofit organization is a great place to start.

There are so many to choose from that it shouldn't be too difficult to find a cause that's important to you. Plus, many nonprofits are willing to build upon your current strengths and provide training in the areas where you're not so strong. If you search online for "volunteer opportunities near me," you'll be blown away by all the various options.

Now, if you're entirely new to the nonprofit world, you might want to check out your local United Way. This organization acts as a fundraising mechanism for many local nonprofits. So, by serving for a season at United Way, you'll not only be introduced to many good causes in your community, you'll have a better idea of which ones might be right for you.

One of the best parts about serving for a nonprofit is they typically have an open-door policy, meaning you can come and go as you please without any real commitment. This is handy when testing the waters and unsure which organization might be the best fit.

That brings me to a significant point. Even though many nonprofits exist, it can be tough to find the right opportunity. In fact, depending on where your talents lie, it may feel impossible at times. For instance, my primary spiritual gifts of perception and administration, along with my management history, mean I would be an excellent candidate to coordinate and oversee an organization's team of volunteers. But I can't simply walk in off the street and expect a director to place me in such an important role, even though I was designed for it and have all the qualifications. Of course, the same will likely be true for you, too. But don't let this discourage you.

Here's a tip you may find helpful. As I already mentioned, it's often necessary to start by working outside your giftings. But as you become more familiar with the organization, identify the person doing what you think you'd be perfect at and ask if you can assist them. Then, once trust has been established, ask this person to help you find opportunities that align with your talents and plan.

Another great place to get started serving is at your local church. If you already have a church home, you probably hear about opportunities to help every single week. But, full disclosure: some churches require you to be a member before serving, at least for roles like working with children or leading classes.

Again, you'll most likely have to settle for doing something you're less than suited for at first. But I promise you, once people understand you can be counted on, you'll be asked to take on more. And that leads us to the next topic—when to say "No."

When to say "No"

When it comes to serving others, there's usually more work to be done than there are workers. And since, by definition, volunteers don't get paid, assignments are typically divvied out to anyone willing to take on the challenge, regardless of their talents or training. Therefore, the person in charge may have acquired their leadership role through attrition rather than their ability to lead. So be prepared to exercise your patience and show a little grace.

Don't forget what we learned in The Parable of the Talents; those who demonstrate ability are often asked to take on more. So, when filling a role that's not in your wheelhouse, it's not a matter of *if* you will be asked but *when*.

I've witnessed, time and time again, volunteers at both churches and nonprofit organizations become stressed out or burned out because they took on assignments they should have never been asked to take on in the first place. Subsequently, many quit prematurely, or worse, they finish their post and vow never to serve again.

This is precisely why having a plan and a firm understanding of your God-given spiritual gifts is so important. It will give you the confidence to stand your ground and say, "Sorry, but I have to say no. It's just not a good fit for me." If we continually take on the wrong roles and refuse to follow God's plan for our lives, sooner or later, we'll find ourselves standing on the corner of "Frustration Avenue and Disappointment Drive."

Oh, and one last thing. If you choose to take on an assignment that doesn't align with your giftings, don't forget to set up some boundaries and outline your "job description," so to speak. More importantly, determine how long you will be expected to serve in that role before you begin. Because chances are you'll soon be longing for a change of seasons.

Seasons

A guy I used to go to church with once used the word season when describing our friendship. He said, "Kevin, I'm glad God has brought us together as friends for a season." Honestly, his comment kind of hurt my feelings because, in my mind, there wasn't a time limit on our friendship.

But as it turns out, he was right. Today, we only talk once or twice a year at best and mostly about business-related things. Apparently, he understood the seasonal nature of relationships a lot better than I did. Likewise, just as our relationships are sometimes seasonal, most divine appointments—like helping someone in need—aren't meant to last forever.

Whether you prefer the label of talents, gifts, aptitudes, or "stuff," the things that make us valuable to others change with each passing day. But even if our talents never changed, our circumstances most certainly would. Therefore, God's plan for our lives will also change accordingly.

For most of us, change is not the sort of thing we look forward to. But the sooner we accept its inevitability, the better prepared we'll be to move gracefully from one season of serving to the next.

Mentoring

Speaking of change, perhaps nothing is more difficult to accept than growing old. Now that I'm on the backside of fifty, I'm slowly but surely seeing the irreversible decline in my physical abilities. So even though my mind tells me I feel great and I'm not that old, I know the seasons are changing.

However, the good news is that while my physical ability to serve others may be declining, my depth of knowledge, wisdom, and understanding is much greater than the average person a generation or more behind me. Therefore, I want to touch on what I believe is perhaps the most impactful and overlooked opportunity to love others—mentoring.

In Chapter 21, I shared with you how my grandfather took me under his wing and confided in me about his business and personal life. This gave me incredible insight, and my time with him was, as they say, "priceless." But still, there was more to our relationship than I could recognize at the time. Just days before Akie died, he started crying while I was visiting him at the nursing home and told me, "I'm sorry, Kevin. There was so much more I wanted us to do."

These were the last words my grandfather spoke to me, and they caught me off guard because I had no idea he felt that way. I assumed I was bothering him by hanging around and constantly asking questions. I had always viewed our relationship as a one-way street, with me doing all the receiving. But looking back today, I can see how I had become his purpose, and truthfully, I'm not sure who was getting more out of the relationship, him or me.

As we grow older and slow down, it's not unusual for complacency and maybe even a little fear and self-doubt to creep in and derail God's plan for our lives. And that's truly unfortunate. Because too often, seasoned individuals, full of knowledge, wisdom, and understanding, fail to see the magnitude of what they have to offer.

My grandfather did what most never do in their final season of life. He lived out his purpose in life by becoming my mentor, and even though I didn't fully understand the significance of it, by playing the role of his student, I was not only being served, I was also "serving" him.

Being Served

This brings up something about loving others that I feel is crucial to recognize. Sometimes, you and I are meant to be someone else's purpose. I don't know about you, but I don't like to be on the receiving end of generosity. I prefer to be the one doing the giving. But who am I to stand in the way of someone fulfilling their purpose and receiving validation from God for a job well done? My point is when someone makes a sacrifice on our behalf and shows us some love, maybe instead of feeling guilty, we should be grateful and honored to be a part of God's plan for their life.

Besides, everybody needs a little love sometimes. And that, my friend, is a perfect segue into our next chapter called *Looking Out for #1*.

CHAPTER 29

Looking Out for #1

Stress is God's way of telling us things have gotten out of alignment…

Throughout this book, I've made bold proclamations like "You need to get a bigger plate" and "Pray for God to open doors of opportunity for you to serve." So I can't help but wonder if maybe you're thinking to yourself, "That's easy for you to say. You have no idea what I've got going on in my life today." If that's how you feel, I get it. Living a five-talent life *does* require sacrifice, and it doesn't change the fact that you still need to bring home the bacon and fry it up in a pan and go out on date nights and get your car fixed so you can load up the kids and drive over the river and through the woods to grandmother's house. Believe me, I understand.

But that's precisely why you can't forget to love on yourself. Now, before you start pushing back and thinking, "Who's got time for that," hear me out. Because loving yourself is more than taking time off work and other obligations. It should also include elements of personal development, which can sometimes feel like the opposite of taking a day off. But stay with me because what I'm about to share is vital to living your best life.

In case this is a new concept for you, let's start with what Wikipedia says personal development is supposed to look like:

- Participate in activities that improve awareness and identity
- Develop talents and potential
- Build human capital and facilitate employability
- Enhance the quality of life and contribute to the realization of dreams and aspirations.

Wow! That almost aligns perfectly with what our goals should look like as servants of God. In other words, much of what's required to double our talents falls under what most people would consider personal development. So rather than feeling stretched, you should look at it as something that "Enhances your quality of life and contributes to the realization of your dreams and aspirations."

Some of the most common categories of personal development include mental, emotional, and physical, which are crucial to our overall health and wellness. But there are two often overlooked areas equally important for anyone hoping to grow in their five-talent faith—spiritual and organizational.

There are four areas that fall under the spiritual and organizational umbrella, and they are setting goals, developing routines, creating margins, and journaling.

Setting Goals

Anyone who knows me knows how goal-oriented I am. I love setting motivational goals. But I'll be the first to admit there've been times when being so driven has done more harm than good. That's probably because, in the past, my goals were focused more on finances and my career.

Then, a few years back, I read a book by Michael Hyatt called, *Your Best Year Ever* which transformed my goal-setting philosophy. Hyatt suggests evaluating your life in these ten areas:

- Intellectual
- Emotional
- Physical
- Spiritual
- Marital
- Parental
- Social
- Financial
- Vocational
- Avocational

Hyatt developed a resource called *The LifeScore Assessment* that goes along with his book. It measures how you're doing in each of the ten areas. If you're interested, you can take this free test at www.assessments.michaelhyatt.com. By doing so, you'll discover the areas where improvement is needed most in your life. This, in turn, will allow you to understand what areas you should focus on for the best results.

Here are a few tips to consider. First, more often than not, it's crucial to set both lead and lag goals. What's the difference? Lag goals are the long-term goals people typically set. For example, "I want to lose 20 pounds this year." This lag goal is "what" I hope to accomplish. Lead goals are "how" we achieve a lag goal. So, for example, an excellent lead goal might be to exercise for 45 minutes five days a week. This practice is even more critical for general goals with outcomes that are difficult to measure.

Second, assess and adjust your goals quarterly rather than waiting until the end of the year. This is especially true for lead goals. Often, whenever we set lead goals, we can't be sure how effective they'll be at achieving our ultimate lag goal. After 90 days, however, you will most likely know whether or not your lead goals are working and need to be adjusted or changed altogether.

Last, and most importantly, write your goals down and keep them where they can continually be reviewed. Even the Bible talks about the importance of writing down goals. With the right goals and motivation, I truly believe this year could be the most extraordinary year of your life thus far.

In Chapter 3, we learned that less than 3% of people write down their goals, and that's sad because there's something magical about putting things down in writing. This may sound silly, but I put my annual goals on a whiteboard in our master bathroom. This way, I can read them daily, and it lets Pam know what I'm trying to accomplish each year so she can give me input and support.

Developing Routines

Years ago, I discovered that my day went noticeably better when I took the time to journal, read my Bible, and pray first thing in the morning. Of course, you would think with a discovery like that, I'd never deviate from this routine. I wish that were the case. But life has a way of derailing our best intentions, and before you know it, we find ourselves spending less and less time on the things we hoped to be doing. Inevitably, this cycle of neglect leads to stress.

Stress is God's way of telling us things have gotten out of alignment, and we need to make some adjustments by loving on ourselves. Now, I'm not talking about grabbing a half-gallon of ice cream, curling up on the sofa, and watching your favorite movie, although that sounds pretty good right about now. There are healthier ways to reduce stress, and one of the best ways I've found is to develop routines.

You might have heard this before, but for most of his adult life, Apple founder Steve Jobs wore the same type of shirt, shoes, and pants every day. Obviously, it wasn't because he couldn't afford a better wardrobe or recognize current fashion trends. Instead, Jobs was putting into practice something Sigmund Freud had discovered decades earlier—we have limited mental energy related to decision-making and self-control.

In other words, an individual can only make a limited number of decisions each day before running out of mental steam. At some point, we give up saying no to bad choices and give in to the things that aren't necessarily the best for us. For me, this primarily falls into the areas of exercise and making healthy food choices. Maybe you've noticed something similar in how you make choices. You start the day off great, but the more stressful life becomes, the sooner you give up on things you'd hoped to accomplish and give in to something you were trying to avoid.

Routines make life more predictable by limiting the number of decisions we make each day. In turn, things are less stressful, and we have more mental agility to face those unexpected decisions that aren't so routine. My daily routines, among other things, include journaling each morning, praying with Pam before she leaves for work, drinking 100 ounces of water, talking on the phone with my best friend, and taking an afternoon walk. Whenever you discover something that lowers stress and leads to a healthier you—physically, mentally, or spiritually—I believe you should fight to make it part of your daily or weekly routine.

Something like drinking 100 ounces of water daily may seem too trivial to be an annual goal, but I kept it on my list of goals until it became a routine. My objective is to repeat something over and over until I do it with little or no thought, similar to how we mindlessly brush our teeth or use our blinkers while driving. When a choice becomes a routine, we no longer use up any of our limited mental energy. This, in turn, increases our ability to take on unexpected opportunities without getting stressed out.

For Steve Jobs, what he wore each day was no longer a choice; it became routine. This practice not only conserved his mental aptitude but also his valuable time. So, in addition to making our lives more enjoyable and predictable, routines save time. And this leads us to our next topic—margin.

Creating Margin

How many times have you seen someone in need and felt "your conscience" telling you that you should help, but you didn't? You wanted to, but you just didn't have the time. I believe what most people call their conscience is actually the Holy Spirit, or God living inside us. If that's true, which should take priority, our own daily agenda or a divine opportunity to use our God-given talents to serve someone in need? When we're walking in five-talent faith, we should expect the unexpected. Now I realize I'm oversimplifying things, but the best way to avoid missing out on unexpected opportunities is to intentionally build some "margin" into your day.

This term is derived from the margin in a book—the blank spaces to the left and right of the printed words. This is where you have extra room to draw a star beside something important or take notes. I like to think of it this way: having some margin in your life is similar to having a large sum of money at your disposal, so when the right investment opportunity comes along, you can seize it. Without factoring margin into your daily schedule, you might have to pass up a divine appointment that equates to burying your talents.

Journaling

I've been journaling actively for over twenty years. When it comes to personal development, It's easily what I'm most passionate about. That's because I consider my journal an altar. In biblical times, the Israelites would build stone altars to honor God whenever something significant happened. Then, whenever they passed by these altars, they would be reminded how God had provided for them and share the stories with future generations. As it became easier for mankind to write history down on paper, altars became less common.

This is why I journal. What started as a simple prayer journal has become so much more. When I journal, I like to answer these four questions:

- What did I do today?
- What did I learn today?
- What am I grateful for today?
- What am I believing for tomorrow?

My favorite day of the year is New Year's Day—when I go someplace all alone and read through my journal entries from the previous year. I'm always amazed at how little I remember about the things I was once so stressed over. On this special day, I'm reminded of how God answered my prayers and provided for me when things felt hopeless. I add commentary about how God turned things around miraculously, and in doing so, I build a written "altar" to remind me and future generations that God is always there for us.

Standing on the Promises of God

When I graduated from college, my father gave me one of my most prized possessions—a small, leather-bound book called *God's Promises for Your Every Need*. Inside the front cover, he wrote, "To my son, Kevin. Use this book as often as you need it, and know that God's promises are for real." In the Bible, God tells us that we can expect specific outcomes if we do certain things. In today's English, we call these promises.

Whether or not you believe in God, He believes in you. He says so time and time again throughout the Bible, and that's why I think every personal development regimen should include reading the Bible—to remind ourselves of what God has promised us. Now, if you don't have a Bible, all you have to do is go online and simply type "God's Promises" into a search engine, and you'll quickly see that God not only believes in you but He's on your side. In this increasingly noisy world, it's never been more important to hear from the One whose opinion matters most.

Before we move on to the next chapter, let me apologize in advance because chances are I'm about to offend some of you—though not intentionally. Many people find their identity in their careers and, as such, get a little defensive whenever someone has something to say that questions the integrity of what they do for a living. So before you turn the page, do me a favor and say to yourself three times, "I'm not going to be offended."

CHAPTER 30

Work is Not a Four-Letter Word

*Whether we're playing to an audience of One or
ten thousand and one it's "why" that matters to God.*

I was waiting in the airport not too long ago—one of my least favorite things to do. I found a Starbucks and got in line to order some tea. Directly in front of me was a young couple also waiting to order. He was about six feet tall, in full army camo with a duffle bag on the floor beside him. She was noticeably shorter, the crown of her head barely reaching his chin. Although she was attractive, she had the appearance of someone who had just rolled out of bed. Acceptable, I guess, since it was only six in the morning.

The soldier had his arms wrapped around his wife, and he must have kissed her on the forehead at least a dozen times while they waited there. Her head was buried in his chest, with both arms wrapped around him in a big bear hug. She was noticeably upset and not at all interested in breakfast or coffee, but he insisted she order.

It was apparent to me he was about to leave on military deployment. I was curious about their circumstances and even thought about asking to pray with them. But I didn't want to rob any of their precious time. So, instead, I got the soldier's attention and asked if he would allow me to pay for their order. He agreed, and I thanked him for his service.

I've bought many U.S. soldiers food over the years, along with others who risk their lives to protect you and me—police, firefighters, and other first responders. I can't help but respect the sacrifices made by folks on the front line. Some jobs seem to command honor and praise—nurse, doctor, social worker, teacher, counselor, coach, etc.

When I was doing preschool photography, I had moms I didn't even know give *me* a bear hug and tell me how wonderful I was just because I got their toddler to smile for their school portrait. It was my favorite part of the job—even more so than the money. And today, as a business consultant, I get more affirmation than I deserve.

Many people choose an occupation out of a desire to serve others. Honor and respect might be one of the perks of such a job, and rightfully so. But that doesn't mean that person would choose the same career if no monetary compensation were involved and their efforts weren't appreciated.

I'm trying to point out that just because my job directly serves people doesn't necessarily mean I'm doubling my talents and fulfilling my purpose at work. Think about it. Not everyone can have a job where they are showered with appreciation. Somebody has to do the thankless jobs like the guys who show up at my house an hour before I'm out of bed each Monday and make my trash magically disappear. Even though I rarely see them and never thank them, they are most certainly serving the families in my community. Moreover, if no one was willing to perform this task, I assure you, a lot more people would die from disease than those killed by terrorism, crime, or fires.

So, that being the case, how is it fair for me to think I'm better than my trash man just because I have a job where people praise me? Obviously, the answer is: It's not. Now, this is going to get a little philosophical, but almost every job, directly or indirectly, helps someone. And wages, if you think about it, are the validation of a job well done. So when you get a paycheck, it means, at the very minimum, you showed up and did a satisfactory job at what you were hired to do.

For example, my lawn-care guy mows lawns for a living—it's his job. When he cuts my grass, he's serving my family and me. But that's not why he shows up. He's doing it for the predetermined consideration of $80. That $80 is his validation that he did his job well.

So, this poses the obvious question, "Can I double my talents in the workplace?" Well, that's a tricky question. You see, there's a hitch in the concept of the workplace being the arena where we double our talents. Because if I serve others but get paid to do so, I'm receiving validation in the form of wages. So, it's at least part, if not all, of my motivation.

Even if I volunteer and sacrifice my time without receiving any pay, there is still a potential problem. Because if I make that sacrifice in hopes of gaining recognition, honor, or praise, I'm still receiving validation in a manner outside of how God wants me to be motivated. In the book of Matthew, Jesus makes this point when He says:

1   *Take heed that you do not do your charitable deeds before men, to be seen by them. Otherwise, you have no reward from your Father in heaven.*

2   *Therefore, when you do a charitable deed, do not sound a trumpet before you as the hypocrites do in the synagogues and in the streets, that they may have glory from men. Assuredly, I say to you, they have their reward.*

3   *But when you do a charitable deed, do not let your left hand know what your right hand is doing,*

4   *that your charitable deed may be in secret; and your Father who sees in secret will Himself reward you openly.*

Matthew 6:1-4 New King James Version (NKJV)

Now, Jesus isn't saying we need to *go all ninja* and run around like Batman fighting evil in the wee hours of the morning. But it's hard to be a servant without people seeing what you're up to, and it's even harder to keep it a secret from the person being served. The key is to play to an audience of One, meaning God is the only person we should try to impress. Look at what Jesus has to say just one chapter earlier in Matthew:

27 *"You have heard that it was said to those of old, 'You shall not commit adultery.'*
28 *But I say to you that whoever looks at a woman to lust for her has already committed adultery with her in his heart."*
Matthew 5:27-28 New King James Version (NKJV)

Jesus turned the world order upside down with statements like the one above. In a time when laws dictated both life and religion, Jesus challenged the status quo by emphasizing that what goes on inside a person's head and heart matters more than simply following the letter of the law. So, my point is it's a heart issue. *Why* we double our talents is more important than *how*.

When we serve others selflessly, it's as if we are saying, "Hey God, I'm so grateful you've given me the talents and opportunity to serve this person. I just wanted you to know I'm doing this to say thank you." To double our talents, we have to serve others, not because we're getting paid to do so but as a way of honoring and praising God, even in the workplace.

Now, don't get me wrong, I'm not implying you should quit your job, apply for welfare, and start working for free. Because once you've embraced your five-talent faith, the workplace can still be an ideal arena to double your talents. I know. I know. You're probably thinking, "Wait a minute, Kevin. You just said all that stuff about consideration and validation..." Yes, that's correct. But most of us work with other people, right? Loving those people may be the opportunity God is waiting for you to seize.

When your attitude shifts from an employee trading time for money to a servant who puts the needs of coworkers, vendors, and even the boss before your own, it's safe to say you're doubling your talents. And often, these acts of love can be carried out without anyone knowing about your sacrifice. So just remember, whether we're playing to an audience of One or ten thousand and one, it's the "why" that matters to God.

When I started working at Martin Signs, Steve Martin had a saying printed on his business cards. Today, that same saying is posted in our lobby:

"The only certain means of success is to render more and better service than is expected of you, no matter what your task may be. This is a habit followed by all successful people since the beginning of time. Therefore, I saith the surest way to doom yourself to mediocrity is to perform only the work for which you are paid."

I encourage our team to treat customers the same way they would want to be treated as a customer—even if it means we lose a little profit here and there. Hopefully, you work in a setting with a similar culture of serving. But if not, remember that there is rarely a situation requiring a career change to fulfill your purpose in life. And I would never suggest taking it upon yourself to be the agent of change in your workplace without ensuring your boss agrees. People have been fired for less.

Remember, when you're "on the clock," your time is the company's time. So, unless you were hired to rewrite the customer service policy, I'd advise you to tread lightly. Maybe you just need to remind yourself why your job is important and that you're genuinely helping folks. Whether you're designing bolts, making bolts, selling bolts, turning a bolt on an assembly line, or talking with the end-user who has a problem with their bolt, I promise what you do is important to somebody.

As Americans, we tend to do a lot of complaining—especially about our jobs. According to *The Conference Board Job Satisfaction Survey* published in *Forbes Magazine,* only 48% of us are happy with our jobs. Whether or not you're directly serving others, if you enjoy your work environment, and like the people you work with, I wouldn't advocate starting over and risking the position and lifestyle you've achieved.

Still, if you're in the majority of workers not happy with your job, by all means, make a change. The bulk of our time awake is spent working. Why waste the better part of your life doing something you don't enjoy? On the other hand, maybe you're not working at all, and you're looking for a job. In either case, it makes sense to get some guidance to ensure you find the right fit the first time. The concepts outlined in this book can help, but much better resources are available.

I am a huge fan of Dan Miller's book, *48 Days to the Work You Love.* I've given it to dozens of people who want to make a career change. Miller has put together an excellent resource to help determine what you'll excel at, who you should work for, and how to land a job you'll love. You can go to www.48Days.com to learn more.

There's a lot of noise today about monetizing our passions and turning them into a career. According to the Small Business Administration, 58% of Americans want to be their own boss. However, only 14% are living out their dream of being self-employed. Before you start feeling sorry for the remaining 44%, remember that the SBA also points out that self-employed Americans tend to work more hours, make less money, and endure higher stress levels than those who work for someone else. If that wasn't bad enough, business owners must face the reality that only half of all new businesses survive the first five years.

Still, many of you are reading this book thinking you've got what it takes to be your own boss, and the only way you'll be truly happy is to take the leap into entrepreneurialism. I've done it right several times and gotten it wrong more than I care to admit. So, take heed before you put in your two-week notice. I first suggest finding resources to prepare you for success. The book entitled *Day Job to Dream Job*, by Kary Oberbrunner, is an excellent place to start. Check it out at www.day-jobtodreamjob.com.

My dad used to tell me, "Whatever you do, make sure you do it in a way so people will miss you when you're gone." He was talking about the workplace, but shouldn't that apply to every aspect of life?

CHAPTER 31

Talent Show

Whatever you do, make sure you do it in a way so people will miss you when you're gone. — Dave McBroom

Even though 87% of Americans own a Bible, more than half admit they've only read a handful of passages or none at all. This is one of the reasons why I chose to write this book. If most Americans have read zero or almost none of the Bible, that's a whole lot of people who've never heard of The Parable of the Talents nor the fact that God created them to live a life of significance through loving others. One only has to look at the increasing number of suicides to understand that people need to hear that their lives have a purpose and God is counting on them.

When I share the story of my journey with others, people often say, "I wish God talked to me." They see themselves as somehow incapable of hearing from God. But nothing could be further from the truth. Television personalities have recently been poking fun at prominent political leaders who've admitted they hear from God. But according to YouGov.com, 38% of Americans admit to doing something in their lives because they believed God told them to.

Believe it or not, God *is* trying to communicate with you. So everyone, not just religious people, can receive validation from God. But even if you *think* you've heard from God, how can you know for sure? How do you know if it's really God talking and not just a combination of sleepless nights and some lousy pizza? That's a great question, but the answer is much less complicated than you might think.

God uses many ways to speak to us, too many to identify them all. Case in point, about 3500 years ago, God once used a talking donkey to influence a King. I'm not making that up—it's in the Bible. So, I think it's safe to assume hearing from God is not limited to written words, sermons, songs, books, or movies. Nevertheless, getting the validation we seek can feel elusive when we need it most, especially today when so many things are fighting for our attention, and we no longer know who we can believe. That's why the Bible is the safest place to turn whenever you're trying to ensure your life is headed in the right direction.

The Bible is God's primary communication avenue when speaking to His children—a.k.a. "us." I like to think of it as a collection of maps or charts that help us set a course and validate our heading in life. When we believe God is trying to tell us something, but we're just not sure, the Bible either confirms or dispels it. It's our primary source for validation.

I hope this book has given you insight into God's plan for your life. But to be completely honest, there are more insightful books about the subject written by folks a lot smarter than me. Regardless, when it comes down to deciding what to believe, you can always confirm what's right or wrong by reading the Word of God.

One thing I've learned by writing this book is just how difficult it can be to articulate matters of the heart, and I can't help but worry I may have lost some of you along the way. So, as we conclude our journey together, I want to take a moment to summarize the material we've covered.

1. We instinctively crave praise.

    God created us to praise, honor, and worship Him, and since He made us in His own image, we, too, crave praise, honor, and worship. Although we tend to describe it using more modern terms like acceptance, respect, acknowledgment, approval, affirmation, or validation. It's only natural that we seek validation from other people. But by doing so, we often find ourselves at one of two opposite ends of the spectrum—disappointed or prideful. And this is why we should focus on receiving validation from God instead.

2. We all have the same purpose.

    Our purpose in life is universally the same as everyone else. It revolves around serving others, and it's what I call "Love 3X": loving God, loving others, and loving ourselves. Of these three, loving others is our primary purpose. It's how we demonstrate our love for God. Serving others is also the primary way we love ourselves because focusing on loving others leads to a happier and more fulfilling life—an "abundant life."

3. We have unique talents.

    God equips us with unique gifts to fulfill our purpose of loving others. The book of Matthew calls these gifts talents, which are most commonly recognized as natural, God-given talents, spiritual gifts, and personality traits. However, the knowledge we acquire, whether formally or informally, along with the wisdom and understanding we obtain from past experiences, is even more valuable. In addition, most of us have been blessed with material possessions and other resources that equip us to bless others. Our talents enable us to help the persons or groups of people God desires us to serve.

4. Come up with a plan.

    Once we recognize our lives have purpose and it involves serving others, it's probably time to move beyond performing the occasional random act of kindness and develop an actual plan. After all, this is our life's purpose we're talking about. Plus, seasons of serving often choose us instead of the other way around. Therefore, if we don't have a solid understanding of the talents God has blessed us with and a plan for how best to apply them, we might just find ourselves doing more harm than good.

5. Choose your passions.

   God may choose our talents, but we choose what we become passionate about. When we decide to pursue our purpose passionately, we have the potential to become great at serving others. However, passions stem from our emotions. So we should remain cautious that they don't take over areas of our lives and become unhealthy—mentally, physically, spiritually, or relationally.

6. Overcome fear and complacency.

   Fear and complacency can keep us from getting out of our comfort zones and taking action when an opportunity to serve others presents itself. And, of course, things don't always go as planned. It takes faith and passion to overcome our fears and resist the impulse to quit or simply do the bare minimum to get by. God has given us everything we need to double our talents. So when we bury our talents and aren't even willing to try, He doesn't take it lightly.

7. Don't run from the past.

   Too often in life, we allow experiences, circumstances, and missed opportunities to define who we are negatively. Our past, however, connects us with others both personally and spiritually, offering unique opportunities to show them some love. When we face the pain of our past and help others going through similar circumstances, we fulfill our purpose and experience healing and growth personally.

8. Expect the unexpected.

   Life rarely goes as planned, but that doesn't mean God doesn't care about us or abandoned us. On the contrary, when walking in five-talent faith and intentionally doubling our talents, God opens the doors to unexpected opportunities to serve. These new experiences bring knowledge, wisdom, and understanding, increasing our ability to love. This is how God takes us from being "faithful over a few things" to becoming "ruler over many." So expect the unexpected.

9. Develop personally.

   We don't know when the next season of our life will begin or what it will look like. Therefore, we need to be optimistically ready to embrace change. Often, this means expanding upon "what we know and what we can do." Adopting practices like goal setting, creating routines, and building margin into our day is a great place to start. But it's even more vital to continually develop our faith by understanding God's promises in His written Word.

10. Do it from the heart.

   The world judges outward accomplishments, but the Bible says God sees our hearts. So even if we do all the right things but do them for the wrong reasons, God may still call us out as wicked and lazy. That means whether we're serving in public or private, at work or home, we should strive to love others for one reason: To praise and honor God with a child-like faith that shows Him how grateful we are for all He's given us.

God certainly *has* given each of us an abundance of talents. As a result, you and I have the potential to make a significant impact on the lives of others. However, most of the time, we don't scratch the surface of that potential, and people suffer because of our apathy. That's precisely why God called the one-talent servant wicked and lazy. Aren't you glad He's a God of second chances? I know I am.

I hope by taking this journey with me; you've become motivated to develop your five-talent faith and to passionately double your talents. You may have moments of doubt and stumble along the way. But I promise you'll soon overcome your self-limiting beliefs and boldly embrace new and unexpected opportunities in a way that'll make your friends and family wonder what's happened to you. Of course, you may not get to witness the fruits of your efforts. But regardless, you'll leave behind a legacy that impacts future generations, I promise. And along the way, you'll find the affirmation, approval, respect, and honor you've longed for.

Just like George Bailey, we may *think* we know what we're going to do tomorrow and the next day, and the day after that. If so, after reading this book, you may think God has bigger and better plans for your life. The truth is God *does* have better plans for you. But they may not be bigger; they might be smaller or more focused. In fact, they might be very similar to where you are today, or they may take you on a journey you never dreamed possible. However, one thing is certain—your life is not some random, meaningless existence. God has a plan for everyone, especially someone like you who's ready to live a life of significance. He doesn't need your help, but he wants it, and He's longing for the chance to tell you, "Well done!"

Applications

Now that you understand your overall purpose and *why* your role here on earth is so vital, it's time to figure out *how* God specifically wants you to double your talents. I understand you may be completely overwhelmed in your current season of life, so the thought of pursuing anything more is daunting. Heck, some of you probably feel like all you do is serve others, and if there's anyone you need to show some love to right now, it's yourself.

But hear me out. Everyone needs a written plan detailing where they hope to be someday. It can be liberating once you've decided to intentionally double your talents, even if you're uncertain when or how you'll reach your desired destination. It's as if God is shining a light in the darkness, directing your path. You no longer question why you are where you are in life because there's a peace validating your decisions and circumstances and, ultimately, your very existence.

With that in mind, I've designed the following applications to assist you in developing a five-talent plan of your own. Depending on the season of life you find yourself in today, some applications will be more beneficial than others. Regardless, I want to encourage you to complete all the exercises because doing so will help you embrace your strengths while overcoming your weaknesses.

Don't forget that our primary objective is to praise and honor God in everything we do. So before you begin, pray and ask God to help you with this process. If you're unsure what to ask for, pray the prayer below:

"Dear God, thank you for equipping me with everything I need to live a life of significance. Your Word promises if I ask for wisdom, you will freely give it. Your Word also

promises that your Son, Jesus, gives me the strength to do anything. So I'm asking you to reveal your plan for my life and help me to carry it out. As I work on these exercises, shield my mind from negative thoughts and give me the courage to look beyond my comfort zone. Finally, Father God, please forgive me for all the times I've failed to use my talents to love others. I give you permission to mold me into who you want me to be so I can serve who you made me to serve. Amen."

The exercises you're about to dive into aren't meant to be quick and easy. So take your time and listen for God's still, small voice along the way. If you need additional help, you're always welcome to contact me. I can be reached by email at kevin@ kevinmcbroom.com, or feel free to call me at 904-599-5997.

Once you've completed the applications and developed your plan, keep it somewhere handy and review it regularly to ensure you've not gotten off course at some point. At a minimum, you should do this annually or following any significant change in circumstances. Oh, and in case you want to take notes, there's a place to do so at the end of the Applications section.

Okay, it's time. So, in the immortal words of my favorite childhood book by Dr. Seuss, "Go dog, go!"

APPLICATION I

—

Spiritual Talents

The first and most crucial step when building a home is to create a strong foundation. If not done properly, it opens the door to potential problems throughout the entire building process. Similarly, pinpointing and understanding your spiritual gifts is the foundation required to build your five-talent faith and double your talents.

Below, I've included an abridged assessment found in Don and Katie Fortune's book *Discover Your God-Given Gifts* (shared with permission from Baker Publishing Group). This application will assist you in determining the motivational gifts God has blessed you with and, subsequently, which serving opportunities you are best suited for.

Remember that the exercise below is merely a portion of the actual assessment, so your results may not be entirely accurate. Nevertheless, this exercise should give you a general idea of how you are spiritually gifted, and you'll need this information to complete the rest of the applications. At a later date, I recommend you take the complete assessment in *Discover Your God-Given Gifts* or choose a similar resource to understand your spiritual gifts better.

Now, before you begin, let me stress the importance of getting things right on this first exercise because it's vital for the remaining applications. So take your time and be completely honest when assessing yourself. Don't answer how you hope to be someday or how you want others to perceive you; when in doubt, ask your spouse or a close friend for input.

1) Using the scoring guide below, write the number that best describes you in the blank preceding each characteristic.

Always = 5 Usually = 4 Sometimes = 3 Seldom = 2 Never = 1

Characteristics of the Gift of **PERCEPTION**
___ Quickly and accurately identifies good and evil and hates evil
___ Easily perceives the character of individuals and groups
___ Boldly operates on spiritual principles
___ Desires, above all else, to see God's plan worked out in all situations
___ Has strong opinions and convictions

TOTAL for PERCEPTION = _____

Characteristics of the Gift of **SERVING**
___ Easily recognizes practical needs and is quick to meet them
___ Has a hard time saying no to requests for help
___ Is more interested in meeting the needs of others than their own needs
___ Shows love for others in deeds and actions more than words
___ Supports others who are in leadership

TOTAL for SERVING = _____

Characteristics of the Gift of **TEACHING**
___ Validates truth by checking out the facts
___ Loves to study and do research
___ Is more objective than subjective
___ Has strong convictions and opinions based on investigation of facts
___ Believes truth itself has the power to produce change

TOTAL for TEACHING = _____

Characteristics of the Gift of **EXHORTATION**
  ___ Loves to encourage others to live up to their full potential
  ___ Views trials as opportunities to produce personal growth
  ___ Accepts people as they are without judging them
  ___ Is well-liked because of his or her positive attitude
  ___ Wants to clear up conflicts with others quickly

  TOTAL for EXHORTATION = _____

Characteristics of the Gift of **GIVING**
  ___ Gives freely of money, possessions, time, energy, and love
  ___ Loves to give without others knowing about it
  ___ Gives to support and bless others or to advance a ministry
  ___ Believes God is the Source of his or her supply
  ___ Likes to get the best value for the money spent

  TOTAL for GIVING = _____

Characteristics of the Gift of **ADMINISTRATION**
  ___ Is highly motivated to organize that for which he or she is responsible
  ___ Will assume leadership where no specific leadership exists
  ___ Is a visionary person with a broad perspective
  ___ Finds greatest fulfillment and joy in working to accomplish goals
  ___ Wants to see things completed as quickly and effectively as possible

  TOTAL for ADMINISTRATION = _____

Characteristics of the Gift of **COMPASSION**
  ___ Has tremendous capacity to show love
  ___ Is attracted to people who are hurting or in distress
  ___ Avoids conflicts and confrontations
  ___ Is ruled by the heart rather than the head
  ___ Rejoices to see others blessed and grieves to see others hurt

  TOTAL for COMPASSION = _____

2) Add up your scores and write down the total for each gift in the appropriate blanks above. The gift with the highest score is your "primary gift." The gift with the second highest score is your "secondary gift." List your primary and secondary gifts below. If you have a tie for your primary or secondary gifts, that's okay. However, it's best to find your top two or three. If necessary, retake the assessment or ask a spouse or friend to help you narrow down your true gifts.

Primary Spiritual Gift/s: _____

Secondary Spiritual Gift/s: _____

3) Read the examples below of how someone might intentionally put their spiritual gifts into practice.

Example 1

Your primary spiritual gift is teaching, and you're passionate about understanding facts and educating others about the truth. You're also a cancer survivor who dreams of making a difference in the lives of those battling the disease. So, you volunteer as a patient advocate for a local hospital.

Example 2

Your primary spiritual gift is giving, and you're passionate about sharing the blessings God has given you, and He's given you a lot. You're not necessarily wealthy, but you've inherited an expansive farm from your parents, with animals, barns, and a guest house. So, you and your husband decide to host a handful of children aging out of foster care. Each week, the children help deliver the eggs and dairy products to local homeless shelters.

Example 3

Your primary spiritual gift is administration, and because your mother is from a small village in Kenya, you're passionate about helping the villagers to overcome poverty. So, you develop a non-profit that pairs start-up businesses in Kenya with American businesses for microloans and mentoring.

Example 4

Your primary spiritual gift is exhortation, and you're passionate about encouraging others to overcome hardship and reach their potential. Because you were physically and sexually abused as a teenager and tried to commit suicide on two separate occasions, you have a soft place in your heart for young girls living in potentially harmful environments. As a result, you travel to schools throughout your state once a week and share your story with all-girls clubs, encouraging them to overcome their fears and openly seek help should they find themselves in an abusive situation.

4) Write your own example of how you might combine past experiences, passions, and spiritual giftings to double your talents and serve others.

_____

_____

_____

_____

_____

_____

_____

_____

_____

_____

_____

_____

_____

_____

_____

_____

_____

_____

_____

Now that you've identified your spiritual gifts and better understand how God has created you to serve, you'll instinctively know when real-life serving opportunities are a good fit for you. Let's be clear, I'm not talking about random acts of kindness, even though I genuinely believe those can be divine appointments. No, I'm referring to sacrificial commitments that alter the order of our lives and potentially impact our emotional and physical well-being.

I hope this exercise has helped you to recognize the value of maintaining the correct heading as you sail along as a servant of God because it only takes one wrong choice to get blown off course. And that leads us to our next application, *Who Do You Love?*

APPLICATION II

Who Do You Love?

Every day, we're presented with dozens of opportunities to serve the helpless, hopeless, and hurting, and yet it seems like there's barely enough time to love on ourselves. For the majority of my life, I was spread too thin to serve others the way I knew I should, and it left me feeling burned out, bitter, and guilty. Can you relate?

That's no longer the case for me today, though, because almost everything on my plate is there intentionally and utilizes the talents God has equipped me with. So now, I'm less likely to get burned out, even while juggling everything else in my hectic life. This is my desire for you as well.

Warren Buffet said, "The difference between successful people and really successful people is that really successful people say no to almost everything." I believe if we want to be happy in life, we must strive to be "really successful" at fulfilling our purpose, and that means knowing when to say "No." When we take on too much, our ability to succeed in life diminishes, and the people and things we care about suffer.

This next exercise is designed to help you identify whether or not the areas where you're currently serving align with your spiritual gifts. You'll start by making a list of who and how you are currently serving. As you do so, let me encourage you not to overlook or discount anything simply because it seems commonplace or insignificant. The goal of this application is to start the process of adjusting your heading so that someday you can reach your desired destination.

1) *The seven motivational spiritual gifts and their definitions from the book Discover Your God-Given Gifts are listed below. Circle your primary and secondary gifts as determined in Application I. If you had a tie for second place, that's okay. Circle that gift as well. But ideally, for this exercise, the fewer the better.*

Perceiver - (in place of prophecy or prophet) one who clearly perceives the will of God.

Server - (in place of ministry or minister) one who loves to serve others. Another appropriate word is "doer."

Teacher - one who loves to research and communicate truth. We almost selected the word "researcher."

Exhorter - one who loves to encourage others to live a victorious life. These are extremely positive people who can equally well be called "encouragers."

Giver- one who loves to give time, talent, energy, and means to benefit others and advance the Gospel. Another word could be "contributor."

Administrator - one who loves to organize, lead, or direct. Other words could be "facilitator" and "leader."

Compassion Person - (in place of mercy) one who shows compassion, love, and care to those in need.

2) *In the lefthand column below, list persons or groups of people you are currently serving. This list will primarily consist of the people you're serving intentionally on a daily, weekly, or monthly basis, like friends, family, co-workers, neighbors, or while volunteering at your church or local nonprofit.*

PERSONS OR GROUPS OF PEOPLE   SPIRITUAL GIFT

_____	_____
_____	_____
_____	_____
_____	_____
_____	_____
_____	_____
_____	_____
_____	_____
_____	_____
_____	_____
_____	_____
_____	_____
_____	_____
_____	_____
_____	_____
_____	_____
_____	_____

3) *In the righthand column above, list which of the seven motivational spiritual gifts you use when serving the persons or groups of people you listed in Question 2. Then, draw a star beside the names of the people you serve using your primary or secondary spiritual gifts.*

4) In the space provided below, transfer the name/s of the persons or groups of people you listed in Question 2 who you did NOT draw a star beside. After each name is transferred below, list any limitations, boundaries, or actions you feel should be implemented to avoid becoming bitter or burned out. Be specific.

_____

_____

_____

_____

_____

_____

_____

_____

_____

_____

_____

_____

_____

_____

_____

_____

_____

_____

_____

_____

_____

5) In the space provided below, transfer the name/s of the persons or groups of people you listed in Question 2 whose name/s you DID draw a star next to. What do you need to start doing, stop doing, keep doing, or become better at to be more passionate about your current season of serving? Brainstorm some ideas below.

_____

_____

_____

_____

_____

_____

_____

_____

_____

_____

_____

_____

_____

_____

_____

_____

_____

_____

_____

_____

_____

_____

_____

_____

I don't know about you, but for many people, this application can be pretty tough. Maybe that's because sometimes we find ourselves serving others in ways that feel more like an obligation rather than one of choice. Whenever we operate outside of our spiritual gifting, we often end up doing things we're either not good at or don't enjoy.

An example of this would be my relationship with my family members. Whenever they need my help, they rarely want me to put on my administrator's hat, even though it's primarily who God made me to be. So, I mostly love and support them in ways that don't come naturally to me.

But there's a positive side when this happens. When obligations require us to love others in ways that stretch us, it's often part of God's plan for personal growth. In fact, the Bible says we should rejoice in our struggles because it helps us grow.

When we embrace the mindset that God is always working on our behalf, we operate in what I like to call "five-talent faith." This faith-filled attitude of gratitude allows us to walk in peace, no matter how uncomfortable things may get from time to time. For me, this is critical. Because when relationships start going sideways, I get tempted to throw my hands up and quit out of frustration, and that's the last thing my family wants or needs.

Okay. It's time for the next application.

APPLICATION III

Thinking Bigger

We've all had dreams that never came to pass. You say to yourself, "Next year, I'm going to…" But for whatever reason, you fail to make it happen. These disappointments, along with the busyness of life, can keep us from dreaming of a better tomorrow, and that's dangerous. Because if you're afraid to dream big, you'll never become who God truly created you to be. Everything great starts with a dream.

Throughout this book, I've argued that we should have a written plan that intentionally utilizes our talents to fulfill our true purpose: to love God by loving others. This next exercise is designed to uncover your potential for greatness and lay the groundwork for developing a success plan.

Even if your plate is full and you feel it's a waste of time to think about things that may never come to pass, don't skip this application. Because odds are, your current season of serving will end someday, and God only knows what lies ahead for you.

A few years ago, I attended a conference where a guy named Mike Kim spoke. I've followed Mike for years. He is a marketing genius, business strategist, and author of the book You Are The Brand. At the conference, Mike asked us to answer three questions that became a vital part of how I approached doubling my talents. These questions can be super helpful in identifying who God wants you to be passionate about serving. Here are the questions:

- *What makes you angry?*
- *What breaks your heart?*
- *What problem do you want to solve?*

One thing that really chaps my hide today is that Redken discontinued the hair gel I've used for the last ten years. Do they not realize what an incredible pain it is to figure out which gel I should replace it with? Of course, I'm not serious. I'm just trying to be funny because these questions are designed to provoke feelings about things much more consequential to humanity than a mere personal inconvenience resulting in a bad hair day.

In this exercise, you will use these three questions to look beyond your limitations and set some big, audacious goals. Unlike when my dad read the book *Thinking Big* and asked me to make a list of self-serving goals, these goals should focus more on the needs of others. Depending on your personality, this exercise may make you uncomfortable and perhaps even melancholy. Nevertheless, I hope you'll leave your comfort zone, bare your soul, and think bigger.

1) Write your answers to the following questions in the space provided below:

When you think about your world today, what makes you angry, and what breaks your heart?

_____

_____

_____

_____

_____

_____

_____

_____

_____

_____

_____

_____

_____

_____

_____

_____

_____

_____

_____

_____

_____

_____

_____

2) *Review your answers to Question 1 and determine which single topic you are most passionate about. Then, in the space below, answer the following question accordingly:*

What problem do you want to solve?

_____

_____

_____

_____

_____

_____

_____

_____

_____

_____

_____

_____

_____

_____

_____

_____

_____

_____

_____

_____

_____

_____

_____

3) If money, time, physical ability, mental ability, and support were not an obstacle, how could you specifically make a difference in the lives of the people impacted by your answer to Question 2? Hold nothing back. If you can imagine it, write it down. You can always add or remove items later. Try to come up with at least five ideas.

4) *Assume you will someday accomplish everything you listed in Question 3. Rewrite your answers in the space provided below. However, this time, list them in the order they would need to be completed. Then, beside each, write how long you think it might take to achieve each item.*

_____

_____

_____

_____

_____

_____

_____

_____

_____

_____

_____

_____

_____

_____

_____

_____

_____

After completing this application myself for the first time, I remember looking over my answers and thinking, "There's no way I'll ever accomplish all of these in my lifetime." Maybe you're feeling the same way right about now. But look at it this way: you're making a plan, which means you've already done more than 97% of the people in this world. Plus, you've completed three of the five applications, so don't stop now; you're more than halfway home.

APPLICATION IV

—

Your Best Life

In Chapter 20, I shared with you what I call my *Best Life List*. Essentially, it's a list of answers to the question, "What do I want my life to look like?" The first time I made this list, my answers were short and to the point, without much thought as to why they were important or how they might impact my life. However, as I've completed this exercise numerous times through the years, I've focused more on the *why* and the *how* behind my answers. This deeper part of the process allows us to move beyond simply filling out a wish list to finding the motivation required for our hopes and dreams to become reality. Subsequently, today, I would describe my *Best Life List* as more of a *Best Life Mission Statement*.

Remember that the objective is less about setting goals and more about defining the habits and attitudes that will help you achieve your best life. If you struggle with the *why* and *how* part, try doing what I do and add the phrase "so I can _____" to the end of each item on your list. For example, on my current list, I have "Be the healthiest version of myself *so I can* do all the things I've listed above." I hope that helps.

Okay, now it's your turn.

1) Envision what your "Best Life" might look like and write it below. You can do so in a short story format or by simply making a list similar to mine. Just be sure to identify why these items are important to you and how incorporating them might impact your life and those around you. We're not talking about some pie-in-the-sky dream list. Instead, this list should be more down-to-earth. Simply put, it's what you think your life could be like someday if things fall into place and go as planned. So, let's begin. How do you want your life to look?

_____

_____

_____

_____

_____

_____

_____

_____

_____

_____

_____

_____

_____

_____

_____

_____

_____

_____

_____

_____

_____

Well, what do you think? I bet you didn't realize how extraordinary your life could look. Striving to fulfill this list is a great way to "love yourself." But I'll let you in on a little secret: it's more than that. When you help others accomplish for themselves the things on *your* Best Life List, it's a great way to serve others. So if you struggled to come up with ways to serve others in *Application III – Thinking Bigger*, keep this in mind, and whenever someone says, "I wish I could do what you're doing," consider helping that person's wish to come true.

APPLICATION V

Your "Well Done" Plan

Now it's time for what I believe to be the most critical step in developing a plan to double your talents and become like the five-talent servant. In this exercise, you'll use your answers from the previous applications to compile a set of 90-day goals and action steps.

Before you begin, let me point out a few things that might be helpful. First, remember our overarching objective is to love God, love others, and love ourselves, or as I like to call it, Love 3X. If you're not sure exactly how to love God, remember that when we serve others by using our spiritual gifts and God-given talents, our actions honor Him. Likewise, when we replace our prideful nature with humility and maintain an attitude of gratitude, our gratefulness is praise to God's ears.

The second thing to remember is that our goals should move us towards becoming a better version of ourselves. This means each goal you set should help you become a better servant, develop personally, live a more abundant life, or all of the above. Just don't forget, it's our efforts to double our talents and not our actual accomplishments that cause God to say, "Well done."

The third thing is to understand that there are different types of goals. One of the most common types is a "Routine" goal. This would be something you hope to do regularly, like every day, weekly, monthly, etc. Another common type is an "Achievement" goal, meaning you hope to accomplish something by a certain date.

The final thing I want to point out is how sometimes what we call a goal doesn't really qualify as a goal. For instance, "Be the healthiest version of myself" is more of a mindset than an actual goal. Goals are rarely effective unless they are definable and measurable, so I have to define what it means to be the healthiest version of myself. For me, that means maintaining a certain weight, following a specific diet, and exercising for a set amount of time and specified number of days. So, be sure your goals are clear and well-defined.

At some point during this process, you'll likely question whether you've got the time and talent to pull all this off. Try to avoid this sort of negative thinking. After all, the applications you've just completed are compiled of things God has placed upon your heart, and like any good father, God wants you to have the desires of your heart. Don't forget God gives us everything we need to accomplish our purpose in life, and He promised never to leave or forsake us. So you won't be going it alone.

Are you ready? Are you excited? Well, I'm excited for you. Let's begin.

1) *Review your answers from Question 4 in Application II – Who Do You Love? Using the action steps you listed in the exercise, create goals you'd like to implement within the next 90 days and list them below. Be specific and make sure your goals are well-defined and measurable. Please remember that it's usually best to share boundaries and limitations with others face to face, and the timing of these meetings may affect your completion dates. So keep your dates realistic and stay flexible.*

2) *Review your answers from Question 5 in Application II – Who Do You Love? Using the action steps you listed in the exercise, create goals you'd like to implement within the next 90 days and list them below. Be specific and make sure your goals are well-defined and measurable. LIMIT THIS LIST TO NO MORE THAN 3 OR 4 GOALS.*

3) Review your answers from Question 4 in Application III – Thinking Bigger. Transfer the first goal from your chronological list below and choose a date you could realistically complete it by. Next, write down one or two goals to carry out over the next 90 days, which will put you on the right path to accomplishing your first Thinking Bigger goal. Be specific and make sure your goals are well-defined and measurable. LIMIT THIS LIST TO NO MORE THAN 1 OR 2 GOALS.

4) *Review your answers from Application IV – Your Best Life, and as you do so, ask yourself what you need to start doing, stop doing, keep doing, or be better at doing for each of your Best Life goals to become a reality. As you brainstorm, write down your thoughts and ideas in the space provided below.*

_____

_____

_____

_____

_____

_____

_____

_____

_____

_____

_____

_____

_____

_____

_____

_____

_____

_____

_____

_____

_____

_____

5) *Using the ideas from your brainstorming session in Question 4, list below the goals you feel need to be implemented within the next 90. Be specific and make sure your goals are well-defined and measurable. LIMIT THIS LIST TO NO MORE THAN 3 OR 4 GOALS.*

_____

_____

_____

_____

_____

_____

_____

_____

_____

_____

_____

_____

_____

_____

_____

_____

_____

_____

_____

_____

_____

_____

_____

Congratulations! You've completed your written plan, and now more than ever, you're ready to begin doubling your talents and hear those validating words, "Well done, good and faithful servant." There's been a lot of research about what it takes to carry out goals successfully, and everyone agrees the most important things you can do are to write them down (which you've already done!) and review them often.

Let's face it: it's easy for our dreams to get pushed to the bottom of our priority list. But I promise, if you get into the habit of reviewing and updating your goals, you'll live a life you never thought possible. I'm old and forgetful, so I keep my goals on a whiteboard in our master bathroom. It helps me stay motivated and lets my wife know how best to support me.

That brings up another recommendation from the experts on how to increase the odds of achieving our goals, and that's accountability. Of course, what works for others may not work for you. So be prepared to experiment until you've figured out which strategies best help you to accomplish your goals. Because, let's face it, "life" has a way of keeping us from focusing on what's most important to us.

Revisiting these applications and updating your goals every 90 days will ensure you maintain the correct heading and keep you from getting blown off course. You can download additional copies of the applications at no charge by going to www. KevinMcBroom.com/HeyGod.

Now go and be a blessing.

A Blessing

On behalf of those you're currently serving and the fortunate folks you will someday serve, I want to thank you for deciding to intentionally love God by loving others. Thank you for choosing to become a history-maker and live a life of significance.

I have a favor to ask. I want to hear about the doors of opportunities God is opening for you. Please reach out and allow me to rejoice with you.

In Old Testament times, whenever someone was about to begin a journey, it was customary for them to have a blessing spoken over them. In this tradition, I'd like to speak this blessing over you,

"May the Father of all creation continue to give you knowledge, wisdom, and understanding. May you always be grateful; praising and honoring God in the good times and the bad. May you continue to double your talents and live a life of significance. May God open the doors of opportunity to you and give you the courage to love, and may your life be filled with peace as you walk daily with the Prince of Peace, Christ Jesus."

Five Steps to Five-Talent Faith

Step 1 – Pray daily for forgiveness, wisdom, and opportunity.

Step 2 – Add margin to your day by saying no to insignificant things.

Step 3 – Continually build upon your gifts and talents.

Step 4 – Stay positive, humble, and grateful.

Step 5 – Seek validation from God, not man.

Jesus?

Pam and I are active at Church On The Rock, or COTR, as the locals in St. Augustine call it. Our pastor, Josh Hersey, never ends a Sunday sermon without explaining how someone can have a personal relationship with Jesus. I feel obligated to do the same, especially since, throughout this book, I've emphasized the need for actions more than I have faith.

Many people think to get into heaven, the good you do on Earth must outweigh the bad. However, the Bible tells us that our actions are merely a reflection of our relationship with God. And even though most people believe in God, not everyone believes Jesus is the son of God. But the Bible says that not only is Jesus the Son of God, He is also the only true path to the Father.

Loving others won't erase your mistakes or shortcomings. Neither will it take away your guilt and shame. That's why Jesus died sinless on a cross—to deliver us from sin and its consequences. Without the actions of Jesus, the ultimate Servant, we would never be righteous enough to have a relationship with the Father. The Bible says, "If you…believe in your heart…and confess with your mouth…you will be saved." (Romans 10:9-10)

If you've never asked Jesus to be your personal savior and you'd like to become a follower of Christ, it's easy. All you have to do is "believe in your heart and confess with your mouth."

Each Sunday, Pastor Josh has everyone in our church pray a prayer together. Even for someone like me, who was "saved" at the age of nine, this prayer means a lot. It reminds me that without a relationship with Jesus, it's easy to get blown off course in life. But for someone "confessing their beliefs" and praying this prayer for the first time, it's the most important decision they will ever make.

"Dear Jesus. I give you my life, all of it. Come into my heart. Forgive me of my sin. Wash me, cleanse me, and make me new. All that I am is yours. In Jesus' name, amen."

If you just asked Jesus into your heart for the first time, I'm so very excited for you. Welcome to the family. I want to invite you to visit www.ChurchOnTheRock.net. There, you'll find lots of online resources to help you learn more about the Kingdom of God. I also encourage you to get involved in a local church to hang out with people who will support you as you discover your new identity in Christ.

Notes

References

Prologue

Capra, F. (Producer & Director), (1946). *It's a Wonderful Life*. United States: RKO Radio Pictures.

Matthew 25 Scriptures

King King James Version (1982). Nashville, TN: Thomas Nelson Publishing.

Chapter 3

Schwartz, D. J. (1959). *The Magic of Thinking Big*. Chatsworth, CA: Wiltshire Book Co.

Tracy, B. https://www.briantracy.com/blog/personal-success/success-through-goal-setting-part-1-of-3/. San Diego, CA: Brian Tracy International.

Chapter 5

Kiyosaki, R. T. (2000). *Rich Dad Poor Dad: what the rich teach their kids about money that the poor and middle class do not!* Scottsdale, AZ: Warner Books Ed.

Schwartz, D. J. (1959). *The Magic of Thinking Big*. Chatsworth, CA: Wiltshire Book Co.

Chapter 6

New King James Version (1982). Nashville, TN: Thomas Nelson Publishing.

Chapter 9

Shellnut, K. (2018). 80% of Americans believe in God. (Blogpost). Carol Stream, IL: Christianity Today.

Claster, B. (1953). *Romper Room.* (Television series). Baltimore, MD: Claster Television.

Chapter 10

Wikipedia contributors (2018). Talent (measurement). In Wikipedia, the free encyclopedia.

Chapter 11

McKay, J. (1961). *Wide world of sports* (Television series). Hollywood, CA: American Broadcasting Company.

"talent." Merriam-Webster.com (2017). https://www.merriam-Webster.com.

Chapter 12

New King James Version (1982). Nashville, TN: Thomas Nelson Publishing.

Fortune, D. and K. (1987). *Discover Your God-Given Gifts.* Grand Rapids, MI: Baker Publishing Group.

Carver, J. (2018). https://spiritualgiftstest.com/

Chapter 13

Flynn, P. (2016). *Will it Fly.* San Diego, CA: Flynndustries.

Chapter 14

Wiley, J. (1978). *Disc Profile.* Minneapolis, MN: Personality Solutions LLC.

Littauer, M. (2006). *Wired That Way.* Ventura, CA: Regal Books

Chapter 15

Grazer, B. (Producer), & Howard, R. (Director). (1995). *Apollo 13* (Motion picture). United States: Universal Pictures

Chapter 17

Steinbeck, J. (1937). *Of Mice and Men.* United States: Covici Friede (Publisher).

Chapter 19

Smith, I. (Producer), & Underwood, R. (Director). (1991). *City Slickers* (Motion picture). United States: Columbia Pictures

King King James Version (1982). Nashville, TN: Thomas Nelson Publishing.

Chapter 20

Smith, I. (Producer), & Underwood, R. (Director). (1991). *City Slickers* (Motion picture). United States: Columbia Pictures

Chapter 21

Wilkinson College (2016). *America's Top Fears 2016* (Blogpost). https://blogs. chapman.edu/Wilkinson/2016/10/11/Americas-top-fears-2016/. Orange, CA: Chapman University

Chapter 23

Littauer, M. (2006). *Wired That Way.* Ventura, CA: Regal Books

New King James Version (1982). Nashville, TN: Thomas Nelson Publishing.

Chapter 25

New King James Version (1982). Nashville, TN: Thomas Nelson Publishing.

Hahn, D. (Producer). Allers, R. & Minkoff, R. (Directors). (1994). *The Lion King* (Motion picture). United States: Buena Vista Pictures

Chapter 26

Doganieri, E. & van Munster, B. (Creators). (2001). *The Amazing Race* (Television series). United States: CBS Television Studios.

Chapter 27

Bearde, C. (Creator). (1976). *The Gong Show* (Television series). United States: NBC Studios, Golden West Broadcasting, & CBS Television Studios.

March of Dimes. (2017). *Miscarriage.* (Website post). https://www.marchofdimes. org/complications/miscarriages.aspx

Chapter 28

Bromberg, I. M.D. (2016). *The Lengths of the Seasons (on Earth)*. http://www.sym454.org/seasons/

Chapter 29

New King James Version (1982). Nashville, TN: Thomas Nelson Publishing.

Baumeister, R. & Tierney, J. (2012). *Willpower: Rediscover the Greatest Human Strength*. United States: Penguins Books.

Hyatt, M. (2018). *Your Best Year Ever*. Minneapolis, MN: Baker Books

Countryman, J. (1995). *God's Promises for Your Every Need*. Nashville, TN: Thomas Nelson Publishing.

Chapter 30

New King James Version (1982). Nashville, TN: Thomas Nelson Publishing.

Adams, S. (Editor). (June 20, 2014). *Most Americans Are Unhappy At Work*. United States: Forbes Magazine

Miller, D. (2015). *48 Days to the Work You Love*. Nashville, TN: B&H Publishing Group.

Kline, D. B. (May 2, 2018). *Survey, Two-Thirds of Americans Dream Of Opening a Small Business*. United States: The Motley Fool

Oberbrunner, K. (2018). *Day Job To Dream Job*. Columbus, OH: Author Academy Elite.

Chapter 31

Kinnaman, D. & Leestone, R. (April 4, 2017). *State of the Bible 2017: Top Findings*. Ventura, CA: Barna Group

Centers for Disease Control and Prevention. (June 7, 2018). *Suicide Rising Across the US*. (Blogpost) https://cdc.gov/vitalsigns/suicide/index.html. United States: National Center for Injury Prevention and Control.

Moore, P. (October 25, 2013). *God Told Me To, 38% of Americans*. (Blogpost) https://today.yougov.com/topics/lifestyle/articles-reports/2013/10/25/god-told-me/. United States: yougov.com

About the Author

Kevin McBroom is a recovering workaholic and serial entrepreneur. He is the founder and administrator of www.BusinessICU.com, a platform serving small business owners. Kevin is passionate about helping overwhelmed entrepreneurs become better leaders and managers, so they can get back to doing the things they love.

Avocationally, Kevin loves listening to live music and being outdoors. He is an avid fly fisherman and enjoys exploring nature while wading in knee-deep trout streams and sandy ocean inlets. Above all, Kevin is a faithful follower of Jesus Christ, a proud father of two sons, Andrew and Isaac, and remains deeply in love with his college sweetheart, Pamela. Kevin and Pam currently call St. Augustine, Florida home.

Work with Kevin

KEVIN McBROOM

- Invite Kevin to be a guest on your podcast
- Invite Kevin to be a guest on your YouTube channel
- Invite Kevin to speak to your organization

Topics Kevin loves to discuss:

Love 3X: Redefining Success. This faith-based keynote emphasizes the importance of finding meaning in life by embracing our God-given gifts, overcoming self-limiting beliefs, and becoming intentional about who and how we serve others.

Astronomical Results: Fitting the square peg into the round hole. This motivational presentation spotlights a simple but practical method demonstrated in the movie Apollo 13, guaranteed to motivate teams, stimulate resourcefulness, and increase productivity.

Business ICU: Exceeding customers' expectations through integrity, communication, and urgency. Winning over customers in the "new normal" is easier than ever before. Now is the time for a renewed commitment to customer service, team building, and community involvement.

www.KevinMcBroom.com

BusinessICU

Integrity. Communication. Urgency.

Business ICU is a business and leadership mentoring program designed to help overwhelmed workaholics:

- Create prosperity by focusing on integrity, communication, and urgency
- Exceed the expectations of customers, coworkers, and community
- Develop leadership skills that attract, develop, and retain top talent
- Establish systems to create predictability and profit
- Build financial freedom through passive income streams
- Create margins of time to live a more meaningful life

Visit www.KevinMcBroom.com/BICU to learn more about Business ICU or to inquire about:

- Being mentored by Kevin
- Scheduling Kevin to speak to your organization
- Scheduling Kevin as a guest on your podcast

Made in United States
Orlando, FL
04 January 2024